CU00375798

Curators of Cultural Enterprise

DOI: 10.1057/9781137478887.0001

Other Palgrave Pivot titles

Thomas Kaiserfeld: **Beyond Innovation: Technology, Institution and Change as Categories for Social Analysis**

Dirk Jacob Wolfson: **The Political Economy of Sustainable Development: Valuation, Distribution, Governance**

Twyla J. Hill: **Family Caregiving in Aging Populations**

Alexander M. Stoner and Andony Melathopoulos: **Freedom in the Anthropocene: Twentieth Century Helplessness in the Face of Climate Change**

Christine J. Hong: **Identity, Youth, and Gender in the Korean American Christian Church**

Cenap Çakmak and Murat Ustaoğlu: **Post-Conflict Syrian State and Nation Building: Economic and Political Development**

Richard J. Arend: **Wicked Entrepreneurship: Defining the Basics of Entreponerology**

Rubén Arcos and Randolph H. Pherson (editors): **Intelligence Communication in the Digital Era: Transforming Security, Defence and Business**

Jane Chapman, Dan Ellin and Adam Sherif: **Comics, the Holocaust and Hiroshima**

AKM Ahsan Ullah, Mallik Akram Hossain and Kazi Maruful Islam: **Migration and Worker Fatalities Abroad**

Debra Reddin van Tuyll, Nancy McKenzie Dupont and Joseph R. Hayden: **Journalism in the Fallen Confederacy**

Michael Gardiner: **Time, Action and the Scottish Independence Referendum**

Tom Bristow: **The Anthropocene Lyric: An Affective Geography of Poetry, Person, Place**

Shepard Masocha: **Asylum Seekers, Social Work and Racism**

Michael Huxley: **The Dancer's World, 1920–1945: Modern Dancers and Their Practices Reconsidered**

Michael Longo and Philomena Murray: **Europe's Legitimacy Crisis: From Causes to Solutions**

Mark Lauchs, Andy Bain and Peter Bell: **Outlaw Motorcycle Gangs: A Theoretical Perspective**

Majid Yar: **Crime and the Imaginary of Disaster: Post-Apocalyptic Fictions and the Crisis of Social Order**

Sharon Hayes and Samantha Jeffries: **Romantic Terrorism: An Auto-Ethnography of Domestic Violence, Victimization and Survival**

Gideon Maas and Paul Jones: **Systemic Entrepreneurship: Contemporary Issues and Case Studies**

Surja Datta and Neil Oschlag-Michael: **Understanding and Managing IT Outsourcing: A Partnership Approach**

Keiichi Kubota and Hitoshi Takehara: **Reform and Price Discovery at the Tokyo Stock Exchange: From 1990 to 2012**

Emanuele Rossi and Rok Stepic: **Infrastructure Project Finance and Project Bonds in Europe**

palgrave▶pivot

Curators of Cultural Enterprise: A Critical Analysis of a Creative Business Intermediary

▶ Philip Schlesinger
University of Glasgow, UK

Melanie Selfe
University of Glasgow, UK

and

Ealasaid Munro
University of Glasgow, UK

palgrave
macmillan

DOI: 10.1057/9781137478887.0001

© Philip Schlesinger, Melanie Selfe and Ealasaid Munro 2015

All rights reserved. No reproduction, copy or transmission of this publication may be made without written permission.

No portion of this publication may be reproduced, copied or transmitted save with written permission or in accordance with the provisions of the Copyright, Designs and Patents Act 1988, or under the terms of any licence permitting limited copying issued by the Copyright Licensing Agency, Saffron House, 6–10 Kirby Street, London EC1N 8TS.

Any person who does any unauthorized act in relation to this publication may be liable to criminal prosecution and civil claims for damages.

The authors have asserted their rights to be identified as the authors of this work in accordance with the Copyright, Designs and Patents Act 1988.

First published 2015 by
PALGRAVE MACMILLAN

Palgrave Macmillan in the UK is an imprint of Macmillan Publishers Limited, registered in England, company number 785998, of Houndmills, Basingstoke, Hampshire RG21 6XS.

Palgrave Macmillan in the US is a division of St Martin's Press LLC, 175 Fifth Avenue, New York, NY 10010.

Palgrave Macmillan is the global academic imprint of the above companies and has companies and representatives throughout the world.

Palgrave® and Macmillan® are registered trademarks in the United States, the United Kingdom, Europe and other countries.

ISBN: 978–1–137–47889–4 EPUB
ISBN: 978–1–137–47888–7 PDF
ISBN: 978–1–137–47887–0 Hardback

A catalogue record for this book is available from the British Library.

A catalog record for this book is available from the Library of Congress.

www.palgrave.com/pivot

DOI: 10.1057/9781137478887

Contents

Acknowledgements

We are indebted to the indispensable and generous help given by the staff and board of Cultural Enterprise Office, in particular Deborah Keogh, Bob Last and Fiona Pilgrim. We are also extremely grateful to Kirsten Beaton, Soizig Carey, Keith Charters, Fiona Chautard, Jacqui Corcoran, David Culbert, Alice Dansey-Wright, Sally Johnston, Lynn Morrison, Louise Murphy, Natalie Neil, Lynne O'Neil, Lowri Potts, Andy Robertson, Carol Sinclair, David Smith, Alison Stockwell, Sandy Thomson, Helen Voce and Isla Wood, and all the other staff who tolerated us so graciously.

Our thanks are also due to the specialist advisers and CEO clients who gave us their time so willingly.

Others who prefer not to be named have also helped us, and we are grateful to them for their co-operation. In the book, we have named only those CEO staff members who were involved in our initial discussion in setting up the study.

'Supporting creative business: Cultural Enterprise Office and its clients' was supported by the UK Arts and Humanities Research Council, grant reference: AH/K002570/1. The authors gratefully acknowledge the AHRC's support for this research.

DOI: 10.1057/9781137478887.0002

List of Abbreviations

AHRC	Arts and Humanities Research Council
CCA	Centre for Contemporary Arts
CCPR	Centre for Cultural Policy Research
CCS	Cultural and Creative Sectors
CEO	Cultural Enterprise Office
CIDS	Creative Industries Development Service
CIFAIG	Creative Industries Framework Agreement Implementation Group
CISP	Creative Industries Skills Partnership
CRM	Client Record Management
COSLA	Convention of Scottish Local Authorities
DCMS	Department for Culture, Media and Sport
EC	European Commission
EU	European Union
GDP	Gross Domestic Product
GNP	Gross National Product
GVA	Gross Value Added
HIE	Highlands and Islands Enterprise
IP	Intellectual Property
IT	Information Technology
NESTA	National Endowment for Science, Technology and the Arts
Ofcom	Office of Communications
PDP	Professional Development Programme
RDist	Relational Dynamics First
SCIP	Scottish Creative Industries Partnership
SDS	Skills Development Scotland
SNP	Scottish National Party
UK	United Kingdom

UN   United Nations
UNESCO   United Nations Educational, Scientific and Cultural
            Organisation
UNCTAD   United Nations Conference on Trade and Development

DOI: 10.1057/9781137478887.0002

1
Researching Cultural Enterprise Office

▶

Abstract: *This chapter introduces Cultural Enterprise Office (CEO), the book's object of study. Based in Glasgow, CEO is situated in the wider UK 'creative economy' policy framework and its Scottish variant. Studies of intermediaries engaged in cultural business support for 'creatives' are rare. How their performance is formed by the wider institutional landscape and shifting ideas and practices has been little examined. Our research has itself been shaped by the current vogue for knowledge exchange between academics and those they research.*

Keywords: creative economy; cultural intermediaries; Glasgow; knowledge exchange

Schlesinger, Philip, Melanie Selfe and Ealasaid Munro. *Curators of Cultural Enterprise: A Critical Analysis of a Creative Business Intermediary.* Basingstoke: Palgrave Macmillan, 2015. DOI: 10.1057/9781137478887.0004.

Why this book matters

This book is about a cultural agency – Cultural Enterprise Office (CEO) – set up to help individuals and very small enterprises working in the 'creative economy'. CEO's central purpose is to make such 'creatives' become more business-like and thereby improve their chances of making a living over the longer term.

CEO is based in Glasgow, a city richly endowed with a wide range of cultural life and a key location for those engaged in creative work in Scotland. In what follows, we have set out to analyse the web of relationships that CEO has with those it advises and assists – its 'clients' – as well as the wider world of government and support bodies – its 'stakeholders'. For the first time, to the best of our knowledge, we have provided a detailed account of the inside workings of this kind of cultural intermediary.

While the Scottish location is undoubtedly significant, how CEO works, the challenges it has faced as an organisation, and how it has been shaped by its wider environment, are of general interest. Other such bodies operate in other places with comparable constraints and with similar purposes. That is because the creative economy has become a centrepiece of public policy in many countries, now being seen by numerous governments as a major engine of contemporary economic growth. So, while we do not argue that CEO is a model for others, there are some general issues that emerge from this case study. We shall discuss these in our conclusions.

Intervention in the creative economy in pursuit of the national economic interest has become ubiquitous, even being adopted as a global model. The quest to reshape the creative base has made use of a wide variety of agencies, bringing a range of different specialisms to bear. Along with the sought-after economic benefits pursued by each particular nation has been the parallel chase for the special prestige that comes with the success of cultural works that achieve attention and esteem. More commonly, though, most official attention is lavished on products that are box-office successes and contributors to the gross national product (GNP). What can be learned from the analysis that follows, therefore, ought certainly to be of direct interest to the various protagonists of the creative economy – governments, cultural and creative industries policy communities, cultural agencies engaged in analogous activities to those of CEO, creative enterprises, and of course, the 'creatives' themselves.

DOI: 10.1057/9781137478887.0004

What makes this study unique is that it focuses on a largely neglected matter: how intervention in the creative field actually takes place, exposing the conditions that underlie a practice that now bears the burden of such high expectations.

In official accounts of the creative economy, which are marked, more often than not, by an unrestrained boosterism, it is normally insufficiently recognised that most creative work is precarious and the livelihoods of those who practice it are often poised on the very knife-edge of viability. This means that 'portfolio' work – the combination over time of diverse ways of making an income – is commonplace in all cultural fields. The consequent fragility of much of the creative economy entails that government's key interest is centred on making creative work more robust. This focus requires setting various measures in train that are seen as suited to the task. Commonly, these interventionist practices include making creatives more business-minded by, for instance, enhancing their savvy about how to organise their finances, helping them to develop new skills, or telling them how they might exploit the intellectual property (IP) inherent in their output.

This is where agencies such as CEO come into the picture because they are integral parts of how governments try to incentivise, manage and sustain cultural enterprises and entrepreneurs in their quest for global competitiveness, as well as other goals. But little has been written about how they work and are shaped by ruling ideas and practices. A key issue for all concerned is just how well such intervention might be judged to work and how the policy landscape is continually rearranged in pursuit of effective leverage and value for money.

Cultural agencies are purposeful intermediaries: on the one hand, they are aligned with the big picture aspirations of national policy-makers intent on increasing the economic value of cultural businesses, and on the other, they are required to meet the highly specific, complex and variegated needs of practitioners. Thus, they are caught between top-down imperatives that aim to enhance performance and bottom-up demands for services by those seeking a route to survival or better, by making a career through their talents. If the role of such cultural intermediaries is really as important as is regularly trumpeted by the retailers of received ideas, then agencies such as CEO ought themselves to escape the fate of precariousness. But intriguingly, it ain't necessarily so, as our account will show.

DOI: 10.1057/9781137478887.0004

Knowledge exchange

Aside from the inherent policy and practical interest of this work, there is a further, more directly academic, context to be noted. Written by British academics working in the UK's research framework, this book has been deeply marked by its own conditions of production. The study undertaken here is an example not only of fundamental research into the role of an intermediary organisation in the creative economy but also of a considered exercise in 'knowledge exchange' between us as researchers and those that we have been researching.

Lately, such an approach has become *de rigueur* in the UK. It has impacted deeply on academic norms. British academics are also currently enjoined to ensure that their research has a non-academic 'impact', a distinct but related imperative embedded in the UK's Research Excellence Framework, the latest official requirement of British academic life.[1] Couple these distinct but convergent demands for demonstrating relevance with the present desire to exploit the creative economy, which looms so large in the British government's thinking, and we have a convergence and combination of two discourses perfectly epitomising the contemporary utilitarian drive in pragmatic planning by the UK Research Councils. A typical definition, offered by the UK Economic and Social Research Council, states that 'knowledge exchange is a two-way process where social scientists and individuals or organisations share learning, ideas and experiences'.[2] Over the past 30 years, knowledge exchange has been increasingly institutionalised in the higher education sectors of North America and Europe, becoming a key mechanism for connecting the business and education sectors; it is also seen as a driver for innovation and economic growth.[3] This raises fundamental questions about super- and subordination in the development of research.[4] To put it bluntly: to what extent can academics pursue their own autonomously generated agendas? To what extent are they problem makers or problem takers?

These concerns are epitomised by our study, which is a 'creative economy knowledge exchange' project, commissioned by the UK Arts and Humanities Research Council for a wider programme of work on that topic.[5] Critical distance needs to be taken from the broader concerns that have shaped the agenda leading to our work. We have needed to steer an unaccustomed path between our own wish to undertake fundamental research into how a cultural intermediary actually works and learning

DOI: 10.1057/9781137478887.0004

how to engage in knowledge exchange with that body and numerous others besides. It is not the idea of knowledge exchange itself that has been the challenge but rather the pace and intensity required and how this has affected the priorities of the research process. We have also, when it is most obviously pertinent, reflected on our roles in the research.

In this study, we are committed to the idea that our research should be accessible and enlightening to those we are studying and, indeed, consider that it might have a wider public interest. We have adopted this stance in line with our own autonomous academic norms and values.

The knowledge exchange agenda, when applied to the creative sector, now mobilises quite significant numbers of researchers – within a range of public, private and third-sector organisations – with the aim of ensuring that they foster its resilience and competitiveness in a volatile global economy. The programmatic approach to knowledge exchange promoted by the UK Research Councils – the carapace within which this study was devised – aligns directly with this goal.[6]

Knowledge exchange certainly does not take an imagined linear form, where the arrow of knowledge might be thought to move symmetrically in opposite directions between the researcher and the researched. The drive to have academics undertake knowledge exchange is coupled with a striking lack of curiosity about what the real experience of applying this requirement might actually reveal.[7] For instance, our unsurprising experience in this present study is that somewhat raw findings are not invariably welcomed and understood as intended by the recipient at the moment at which they are delivered. Moreover, there is no doubt that practising knowledge exchange in a research project affects the frequency and intensity of researchers' dealings with those who are being researched. Such complexity means that the new normative emphasis has a major impact on how research needs to be planned, managed and executed.

Our aim throughout our project was to inform CEO's own practice and ideas by regularly imparting to the staff, as nearly as possible in real time, what we were learning about them while we were in the process of finding things out. While the added effort of organising knowledge exchange events competes directly with the time available for research, the pursuit of dialogue in this form certainly does not entail telling those whom we are researching what they want to hear – nor should it. Rather, it means keeping a critical distance, while at the same time creating spaces in which we can present our analyses for relatively dispassionate

DOI: 10.1057/9781137478887.0004

debate and, at times and quite rightly so, disagreement by those who do not recognise the picture that is being painted of them, or see it as an unflattering likeness.

Having an Arts and Humanities Research Council (AHRC) grant permitted the research team to make 'a gift' of our funded time to CEO in exchange for access. However, although finding the door fully open to fieldwork offers exceptional advantages, it also requires very careful management of expectations throughout the life of the project.[8]

The far-reaching challenge of doing this kind of work has not yet been fully addressed by research funders, universities or indeed, by academics themselves. Given our immersion in this approach, we see the present work as a contribution to what is increasingly shaping up as a crucial debate about the autonomy of academic life, not just in the UK but wherever the knowledge exchange agenda is being embraced.

About this book

As will be clear, this short book is concerned with the process of organised intermediation between those engaged in creative work and the wider policy and institutional framework in which that occurs. We are interested in the kind of specialised knowledge that is mobilised by those working in an agency such as CEO. Surprisingly, as discussed in Chapter 2, the operations of such bodies as CEO have been largely neglected by academic research.[9] Although there is a small body of related work, thus far nothing has combined research into this kind of cultural intermediary with the pressure of managing knowledge exchange as part of the research process itself.

To that end, we have set out to anatomise the system of beliefs and working practices of one exemplary case to which we have had exceptional access. While our example is undeniably Scottish, Scotland's particular cultural policy discourse and the country's home-grown agencies' approach to the creative economy have been deeply shaped by British ideas and practices, as well as influenced by the movement of key personnel across the border. If some highly specific features characterise our chosen case, we are confident that it is not untypical of what can be found elsewhere in the UK. Moreover, in various ways CEO may also be compared to bodies of similar scale and purpose at work in other national contexts.

DOI: 10.1057/9781137478887.0004

The rest of this book

In Chapter 2, we show how the 'creative economy' became a central plank of UK cultural policy, from the New Labour government (1997–2010) to the Con-Lib Dem coalition government (2010–2015). Both the globalisation of this discourse and its localisation in Scotland are described. The centrality of the creative economy for Scottish cultural policy under both the Lab-Lib coalitions (1999–2007) and the Scottish National Party (2007 to date) is analysed, with particular attention paid to the common political ground regarding the present institutional landscape. CEO is situated in the context of a discussion of current analyses of cultural intermediaries and of cultural entrepreneurship.

Chapter 3 outlines the evolution of Cultural Enterprise Office over 15 years, tracing its development from the initial feasibility study in 1999, through its launch and four phases of operation. We describe the shape of the organisation and its main business support activities during our fieldwork (2013–2014). We address the role of institutional narrative, CEO's changing geographic remit, the way the organisation has drawn on and modified operational models from elsewhere and how it has intersected with and adapted to the existing local and national business support infrastructure. We argue that the quest for survival has required CEO to continually adapt, re-orientating towards different sources of funding and responding to current policy trends.

Chapter 4 takes a close look at CEO's business support practices, examining how the central ethos of the organisation is expressed through day-to-day client interactions and the language in which business advice is delivered and discussed. We identify three core values underpinning the delivery of advice and support to clients: being bespoke, being non-judgemental and taking a coaching-centred approach to supporting clients. We next consider how staff have used the idea of 'client journeys' to conceptualise trajectories through CEO's service and the business world. Finally, we consider the impact on organisational values of the introduction of structured programmes, arguing that these have introduced new languages and different styles of interaction to CEO, reshaping the idea of 'being bespoke'.

In Chapter 5, we address CEO's strategic development during 2013–2014, aided in part by funding devoted to capacity building. In a bid to future-proof the organisation and remain relevant within an increasingly competitive business support landscape, CEO's leadership restructured

DOI: 10.1057/9781137478887.0004

the organisation, began to develop critical independent research into the sector, and sought to reimagine models of digital and physical service delivery. Ultimately, the bid for further Creative Scotland funding to enable more ambitious plans to be pursued was unsuccessful, resulting in the decision to move on by CEO's Director. This chapter explores the development of new goals when their realisation was actually considered to be feasible, considers the internal transformations we observed CEO undergo as it attempted to ready itself for this next planned phase, and finally reflects on the continuing tension between serving and attempting to shape the top-down policy agenda.

Chapter 6 concludes this book. We argue that support for the creative economy operates within a largely unchallenged set of assumptions, including the need for intervention. However, given that policy makers evidently think that bodies such as CEO are important for pursuing national goals, too little attention has been paid to cultural agencies' often precarious conditions of existence. Our study has shown that, irrespective of contemporary political change, Scottish creative economy policy has remained highly dependent on UK initiatives and ideas. Moreover, the cross-border transfer of people and practices has also been important in establishing commonalities of approach. These, however, should not obscure the continuing importance, specificity and impact of place for the functioning of cultural business support, and not least the role of the local funding regime in shaping and reshaping its periodically changing mission.

Notes

1   'The Research Excellence Framework 2014', The Research Excellence Framework, accessed 9 March 2015, http://www.ref.ac.uk/.

2   'The benefits of collaboration', Economic and Social Research Council. accessed 9 March 2015, http://www.esrc.ac.uk/collaboration/knowledge-exchange/.

3   Fumi Kitigawa and Claire Lightowler, 'Knowledge exchange: a comparison of policies, strategies, and funding incentives in English and Scottish higher education', *Research Evaluation* 22 (2013): 1–2.

4   As space does not permit us to take the matter further here, we simply note this point.

5   'Creative Economy Knowledge Exchange Projects', Arts and Humanities Research Council, accessed 9 March 2015, http://www.ahrc.ac.uk/What-

DOI: 10.1057/9781137478887.0004

We-Do/Strengthen-research-impact/Knowledge-Exchange-and-Partnerships/
Pages/Creative-Economy-Knowledge-Exchange-Projects.aspx.

6   Philip Schlesinger, 'Expertise, the academy and the governance of cultural
     policy', *Media, Culture and Society* 35 (2013): 27–35.

7   Philip Schlesinger, Melanie Selfe, and Ealasaid Munro, 'The Supporting
     Creative Business project and the politics of managing ethnographic
     teamwork' (paper presented at the International Conference on Cultural
     Policy Research, Hildesheim, 9–12 September 2014).

8   Our AHRC Creative Economy Knowledge Exchange Project was initially
     a one-year project, but because of the knowledge exchange component in
     practice we found it impossible to complete the work in 12 months and had to
     find the resources to keep it going, beyond the grant awarded.

9   For exceptions, see: Justin O'Connor, 'Intermediaries and imaginaries in the
     cultural and creative industries', *Regional Studies* 49 (2013); Justin O'Connor
     and Xin Gu, 'Developing a creative cluster in a postindustrial city: CIDS
     and Manchester', *The Information Society: An International Journal* 26 (2010);
     Doreen Jakob and Bas van Heur, 'Editorial: taking matters into third hands:
     intermediaries and the organization of the creative economy', *Regional Studies*
     49 (2015); Keith Negus, 'The work of cultural intermediaries and the enduring
     distance between production and consumption', *Cultural Studies* 16 (2002);
     Sean Nixon and Paul du Gay, 'Who needs cultural intermediaries?', *Cultural
     Studies* 16 (2002): 498.

DOI: 10.1057/9781137478887.0004

2
Nation, State and Creative Economy

Abstract: *This chapter shows how the 'creative economy' became a central plank of UK cultural policy, from the New Labour government (1997–2010) to the Con-Lib Dem coalition government (2010–2015). Both the globalisation of this discourse and its localisation in Scotland are described. The centrality of the creative economy for Scottish cultural policy under both the Lab-Lib coalitions (1999–2007) and the Scottish National Party (2007 to date) is analysed, with particular attention paid to the common political ground regarding the present institutional landscape. Cultural Enterprise Office is situated in the context of a discussion of current analyses of cultural intermediaries and of cultural entrepreneurship.*

Keywords: creative economy; cultural entrepreneurship; cultural intermediaries; cultural policy; Scottish Government; UK Government

Schlesinger, Philip, Melanie Selfe and Ealasaid Munro. *Curators of Cultural Enterprise: A Critical Analysis of a Creative Business Intermediary.* Basingstoke: Palgrave Macmillan, 2015. DOI: 10.1057/9781137478887.0005.

DOI: 10.1057/9781137478887.0005

Cultural policy and the creative economy

Contemporary public policy in the UK is overwhelmingly focused on how culture generates revenues for the national economy in the context of global trade. Take, for instance, the UK Government's *Creative industries economic estimates 2015*. These set out 'to measure the direct economic contribution of the Creative Industries to the UK economy' and use what has become an orthodox definition of those industries by the Department of Culture, Media and Sport (DCMS) as having 'their origin in individual creativity, skill and talent and which have a potential for wealth and job creation through the generation and exploitation of intellectual property'.[1]

Questions and caveats about how the gross value added (GVA) to the British economy is calculated do not characteristically find their way into media discourse. Nor indeed, do queries figure in the public domain about what the boundaries of the creative economy are, or what might be the occupations that are held to constitute it.[2] Rather, it is the headline figures of rampant economic success that are the prime focus of attention.

According to the *Estimates*, in 2013, one in 12 of UK jobs was in the creative economy whereas the creative industries accounted for 5.6 per cent of total UK jobs. Moreover, at £76.9bn in 2013, the creative industries evidently accounted for 5.0 per cent of the UK economy's turnover.[3] In similar vein, it has become commonplace for British governments to focus primarily on the economic value of culture and the role that the UK's cultural riches play in attracting tourism. A report commissioned by Arts Council England, delivered in 2013, estimated that culture was worth £5.9bn per annum to the UK economy, with ancillary tourist spending of £856m per annum.[4]

Figures such as these, whether entirely credible or not, are the common coinage of public debate throughout the UK, as much so in the devolved capitals of Edinburgh, Cardiff and Belfast as in London. For an example of how Edinburgh bangs the same drum, consider the arguments about the creative economy presented by the Scottish Government in support of independence. Scotland's creative industries were said to have a turnover of £4.8bn in 2010 and to have contributed £2.7bn to GVA. The Scottish creative industries were reported as employing 64,000 people in 2011, with the creative industries accounting for 5 per cent of Scotland's exports in 2011.[5]

DOI: 10.1057/9781137478887.0005

There is, therefore, a consistent message whatever the official source. But when it comes to talking about culture, where does this prevalent economism come from?

The advent of the 'creative economy'

Ever since the late 1990s, British policy makers, academic analysts and consultants have identified the 'creative industries' as a key driving force in the national economy.[6] The dominant line of argument has tended towards uncritical support for the economic exploitation of culture in the pursuit of competition in global trade. In this context, the tradable value of intellectual property rights has taken centre stage, setting the scene for much consequent policy-making and debate. In Britain, in recent years, there have been two major inquiries addressing these questions. According to Andrew Gowers, reporting in 2006:

> In the modern world, knowledge capital, more than physical capital, drives the UK economy. [...] The ideal IP system creates incentives for innovation without unduly limiting access for consumers and follow-on innovators.[7]

Creative industries are identified as a key sector of the 'knowledge based industries' and creative expressions are seen as value-creating, as subject to intellectual property rights and as needing protection from counterfeit goods and piracy.[8] Reporting in 2011, Ian Hargreaves started from the similar proposition that IP policy 'is an increasingly important tool for stimulating economic growth' within a highly competitive global economy. The creative economy was even more central to the analysis, with facilitating the growth of digital creative firms singled out as an imperative.[9]

Given the dramatic pace of change occurring in the development of information and communications technologies, the 'digital economy' – which, as may be seen from the Hargreaves Report, is not always conceptually distinct from the 'creative economy' – has become a major focus of discussion, not least in terms of how the digitisation of cultural content is impacting on the business models of cultural firms faced with new challenges in distribution and consumption. The producers of music, books, newspapers, films and television programmes have all been required to think afresh about their business models.

With government ministers worldwide talking up the capabilities and talents of their own 'creative nation', a variety of forms of state and

DOI: 10.1057/9781137478887.0005

other public intervention have assumed increased pertinence. Typical measures have included investing in 'human capital', creating special agencies to support cultural producers in developing their business and technological skills, using fiscal measures to promote given industries, and embarking on culture-led urban regeneration. The credibility of evidence about the importance of the 'creative economy' has been questioned and indeed, economistic conceptions of culture have been denounced, but the counter-blasts have yet not displaced a framework of thought that has now achieved the status of global orthodoxy.[10]

The economisation of culture has undoubtedly achieved huge prominence in British official discourse. The developments that led to this state of affairs have been widely discussed. Public policy arguments about the supposedly transformative significance of the creative industries were first most fully developed in the UK, notably under the New Labour government elected in 1997, led by Prime Minister Tony Blair. The ideas that then came into play were the outcome of several lines of filiation with an extensive hinterland both in social science and in earlier public policy interventions.[11]

In the UK, cultural industries policies were first developed at a local level, notably by Labour Party-run councils in pursuit of urban regeneration to counter the de-industrialisation accelerated by the Conservative government policies of Margaret Thatcher.[12] It was around this time that many of the tropes so familiar today developed. The 'city of culture' – Glasgow being a signal, early British example of a 'European City of Culture' – became a prime locus for building up 'clusters' of 'cultural enterprises'.[13] This rather leaden terminological repertoire has become thoroughly normalised, not least through the consistent effort undertaken by New Labour to develop a political language that embodied a particular worldview.[14]

The UK Government's *Creative industries mapping document* managed to achieve widespread influence in international academic and policy circles. The formulation cited at the start of this chapter is now almost two decades old. Aside from proposing, as we have seen, individual creativity, skill and talent, wealth and job creation, and intellectual property as the linchpins of its approach, the DCMS's designation of the creative industries went as follows:

> These have been taken to include the following key sectors: advertising, architecture, the art and antiques market, crafts, design, designer fashion, film, interactive leisure software, music, the performing arts, publishing, software and television and radio.[15]

DOI: 10.1057/9781137478887.0005

The core focus of the *Mapping document* was 'to recommend steps to maximise the economic impact of the UK creative industries at home and abroad'.[16] New Labour used the aggregation of discrete sectors to create a single object of policy. Nicholas Garnham has suggested that this involved repositioning 'culture' as a high-growth sector by linking the so-called creative industries with the 'information economy'.[17] It has proven to be a persuasive and durable formulation. Nevertheless, we should note that the list of 13 industries initially identified is arbitrary: we may readily find different lists proposed by others, as well as a gamut of conceptual refinements relating, for instance, to which are to be judged core or peripheral industries.[18] Second, the DCMS's approach was based in cultural economic nationalism, which has accounted in no small measure for its widespread appeal around the globe. Third, by making the exploitation of intellectual property so crucial, cultural value has been subordinated to economic value. Fourth, while there has been considerable rhetorical success in promoting the creative industries, in practice the continuing diversity and specificity of different sectors makes overall policy-making rather difficult.

New Labour's cultural policies have been a topic of some debate. Some have criticised them as broadly 'neoliberal'.[19] To resume David Harvey's useful characterisation:

> Neoliberalism is in the first instance a theory of political economic practices that proposes that human well-being can best be advanced by liberating individual entrepreneurial freedoms and skills within an institutional framework characterized by strong private property rights, free markets and free trade. The role of the state is to create and preserve an institutional framework appropriate to such practices.[20]

In their study of New Labour's cultural policies, David Hesmondhalgh and his colleagues have suggested that these were not 'neoliberal in any coherent sense of the word' because social objectives were foregrounded and that among their innovations were support for free access to museums, increased corporate sponsorship of the arts, encouragement of the principles of new public management, and a focus on the expansion of the creative industries.[21] Certainly, New Labour's interventionist approach to culture legitimised cultural spending by foregrounding culture's contribution to both economic and social goals. But increased economic competitiveness was of especial importance, not least the contribution it might make to the regeneration of the UK's post-industrial cities. Strikingly, after Labour's 13 years in office under Tony Blair and his

DOI: 10.1057/9781137478887.0005

successor, Gordon Brown, the Conservative-Liberal Democrat coalition that succeeded Labour at Westminster in 2010, led by David Cameron, largely maintained the same approach to the creative industries.[22]

The successor idea to the creative industries is that of the 'creative economy', which also affords a pivotal position to intellectual property. A small bevy of writers close to the policy action have acted as popularisers of official discourse while also being purveyors of marketable expertise.[23] For instance, John Howkins, a consultant well connected in policy, communications and academic research circles, was one of the first to write about the creative economy, like others selecting his own favoured list of what counted as a relevant sector.[24] Part and parcel of the prevailing orthodoxy, his analysis lays emphasis on intellectual property and its key role in 'the global battle for comparative advantage'.[25] For Howkins, as for others, the prime case for taking creativity seriously is that it has an economic dimension and that it should therefore be regarded as 'a substantial component of human capital'.[26]

These largely instrumental views have been widely propagated. In the European Union (EU), for instance, while not all member states have taken up the creative economy cause with equal enthusiasm, by degrees the European Commission (EC) has been won over to treating it as of central importance. The creative and cultural industries are at the heart of the European Agenda for Culture. This is part of the framework of the EU's Lisbon strategy for jobs and growth, originally set out in March 2000. Interventions in the cultural field were subsequently rebadged as Creative Europe, which is described as 'supporting Europe's cultural and creative sectors' (CCS).[27] Creative Europe's goals are intended to address the challenge of globalisation and to enable the sectors concerned to achieve their economic potential. There is an important nuance in the designation of 'CCS', which avoids talking solely about the creative industries and carefully acknowledges the emphasis placed on culture in key member states. The EC maintains that the CCS represent 3.3 per cent of European GDP and employ 6.7 million people, 3 per cent of total employment. The EC is just as interested as the UK Government in the economic impact of the creative economy, with a feasibility study under way to explore how to collect better data.[28]

The de facto globalisation of the creativity agenda has been evident in the UN's successive *Creative economy reports,* the first of which, in 2008, went so far as to style the creative economy as 'a new development paradigm', linking it to sustainable development.[29] This coexists with a

DOI: 10.1057/9781137478887.0005

distinctive stance on the question of cultural value, as it is maintained that 'support for creative domestic industries should be seen as an integral part of the promotion and protection of cultural diversity'.[30] *The Creative economy report 2008* focused attention on intellectual property rights, in keeping with the work of the World Intellectual Property Organisation – like UNESCO and UNCTAD, a UN agency. The emphasis has been on what are called the 'core' copyright industries, namely those 'that produce and distribute works that are protectable under copyright or related rights'.[31] In the course of a decade creative economy thinking had become a protean development ideology.

It is hardly surprising then, that Terry Flew has recently distinguished several policy variants: those of the EU, as well as the distinctive approaches taken in the US, East Asia, China, and Australia and New Zealand.[32] Diverse types of political regime, levels of economic development and the history of institutions all play a role in shaping given policy frameworks. And, of course, there are interconnections between each of these variants, as effected by the global circulation of ideas, the border-crossing work of consultants and advisers, and international collaboration.

In short, today's dominant ideas about managing culture in the interests of the national economy were first minted in London. Creative industries thinking has circled the globe and captivated many policy makers worldwide. At the heart of the official British vision of creativity has been the harnessing of culture to the growth of the national economy coupled with a grandiose post-imperial design to make the UK the 'world's creative hub'. Having captured the high ground and set an agenda among both academics and policy-makers, the existence of 'the creative economy' has become a compelling, continually reproduced proposition. Embedded in research programmes and institutionalised in centres, with some writers calling for the creative economy to become a major focus of innovation policy,[33] it has become increasingly difficult to stand back and raise critical questions.

Most often, but not invariably, cultural policy comes under the purview of sovereign states, such as the United Kingdom. It therefore unavoidably and centrally involves public institutions. In the UK, the political focus of much explicit policy-making is the Secretary of State for Culture, Media and Sport together with his or her department, the DCMS. A prominent echo chamber for this policy world in the House of Commons is the Select Committee on Media, Culture and Sport.

DOI: 10.1057/9781137478887.0005

Beyond the Westminster-Whitehall axis, but highly dependent on its machinations, are various kinds of public agency that intervene in the cultural domain, such as Arts Council England and the British Film Institute. These are complemented by a veritable bevy of national bodies ranging from the British Museum, the Tate and the BBC to the London Philharmonic and the National Theatre, and many more besides. Such institutions constitute the highly visible, traditional official apparatus of British national culture.

So far as the creative economy is concerned, during the heyday of New Labour, some new bodies were invented to address the changing media, communications and innovation landscape. The UK Film Council was set up in 2000 with the idea of bringing 'sustainability' to the British film industry.[34] Ofcom, a new 'converged' regulator for the communications sector, was established in 2003, to supersede bodies that had dealt separately with broadcasting, telecommunications and wireless. This was also the moment when NESTA, the National Endowment for Science, Technology and the Arts, was established. In fact, it was at the very head of the reformist wave. It was set up in 1998 as a body intended 'to support and promote talent, innovation and creativity in the fields of science, technology and the arts'.[35]

NESTA's formation is of particular relevance for this study, as its thinking about innovation has been influential and has been embedded in the programmes developed by CEO. As Kate Oakley and her colleagues point out, NESTA's trajectory incorporated New Labour's creative economy policy 'under which an early enthusiasm for supporting small cultural businesses was replaced by the discourse of creativity and innovation'. The original NESTA cultural policy, they maintain, shifted from a concern 'with culture in favour of a focus on economic growth'.[36] They argue that in line with the DCMS's emphasis on IP as 'the engine of economic growth in a knowledge-based economy [...] this was to become the understanding of IP that NESTA promoted'.[37] Over time, NESTA became increasingly focused on the linkage between innovation and economic growth, positioning itself as an 'innovation think tank' influencing policy-making.[38] NESTA's connection with our research is most evident in its 'becoming "a hub for the innovation community", running seminars, lectures and networking events, commissioning research from third parties'.[39] The transfer of NESTA's ideas through specific programmes, and the movement of particular individuals through the support infrastructure, as we shall see, has exerted a

DOI: 10.1057/9781137478887.0005

profound – but little analysed – influence over the ideas and practices of a body such as CEO.

From the UK to Scotland

Sovereign statehood is by no means essential for a cultural policy to be autonomously pursued. Scotland is a nation without a state, although it did have a sovereign political existence until 1 May 1707 when it was incorporated into the United Kingdom of Great Britain.[40] As is well known, on 18 September 2014, Scotland held a referendum to decide whether or not it should become an independent country or remain in the UK. The electorate decided not to seek separate sovereignty and in the immediate wake of what was a closely-fought campaign, the Smith Commission was set up to set out the terms for the next stage in Scotland's devolutionary journey towards what is variously called 'devo max' or 'home rule'.[41] In January 2015, the draft clauses of a Bill setting out new proposed powers intended to redefine Scotland's future relationship with the rest of the UK were published.[42]

The Scottish Government in Edinburgh, presently in the hands of the Scottish National Party (SNP), has made it clear that for it too, a creative economy is important. This was part of the case made for independence.[43] In many respects, the economic dimensions of culture have become more important, not least after the precipitous loss of credibility by the major Scottish banks, the rapid collapse of oil revenues – a linch-pin of the economic case for independence – which fell by 50 per cent between June 2014 and January 2015, and the consequent need to diversify Scottish sources of income generation. At the heart of the SNP's vision for an independent Scotland has been the harnessing of culture to the growth of the national economy. Despite targeted attention from government, the Scottish creative economy contracted between 2011 and 2013, by contrast with the overall growth observed across the UK.[44]

Under the present politically contested constitutional arrangements, cultural policy is a devolved power falling under the aegis of the Scottish Government and Scottish Parliament. This competence was set out in the Scotland Act 1998 in phase one of devolution. Until the independence referendum, the model for devolution's phase two was embodied in the Scotland Act 2012, which – despite pressures from the SNP – did not expand the scope of cultural policy to include broadcasting. The 'reserved'

DOI: 10.1057/9781137478887.0005

powers over broadcasting by Westminster have been a major bone of contention for the SNP.[45] Although the Smith Commission's recommendations did not recommend that broadcasting become a devolved power, some significant changes were proposed. It was proposed that the Scottish Government and Scottish Parliament would have a formal consultative role in the BBC's Charter Review, with the BBC also having more formal accountability to the Scottish Parliament regarding Scottish matters. A formal consultative role for the Scottish Government and Scottish Parliament in respect of the communications regulator Ofcom's strategic priorities in Scotland was also proposed, with similar formal accountability to the Scottish Parliament as that indicated for the BBC. Scottish ministers were to have the power to appoint a Scottish member to the Ofcom Board.[46]

The extent to which broadcasting has been a contentious issue between Edinburgh and London has tended to divert the eye from the extensive state apparatus that Scotland possesses in the cultural field. The sheer extent and density of Scotland's distinctive institutional world is at least in part a legacy of its original statehood and its long-standing, periodically renegotiated forms of autonomy within the United Kingdom.[47] Despite not being a sovereign state, there is an official Scottish cultural policy apparatus, comparable to that of the UK, but on a lesser scale. There is a Cabinet Secretary for Culture and External Affairs and a Culture Division in the Scottish Government as well as an Education and Culture committee in the Scottish Parliament. And just as in London, there are the classic, high-cultural institutions typical of a contemporary European nation state: the National Museums and Galleries of Scotland, the National Library of Scotland, the Scottish National Orchestra, Scottish Ballet, Scottish Opera, the National Theatre of Scotland. To expand on Michael Billig's neat metaphor, such nominal repetitions not only 'flag the nation' but also muster resonant massed pipes and drums to sound the distinctiveness of the national dimension.[48]

The political landscape in Scotland has seen substantial upheaval in the last two decades. The Scottish Parliament – Holyrood – was established in 1999, following the devolution referendum of 11 September 1997. For its first eight years, a Labour-Liberal Democrat coalition ruled Scotland, and the close connections between the Labour Party at Holyrood and Westminster ensured extensive alignment with prevailing policies south of the border, including the new focus on the creative industries. In 2007, a minority SNP Government succeeded the two-term

DOI: 10.1057/9781137478887.0005

Lab-Lib coalition in Scotland. In 2011, the Nationalists formed their first majority government. If there has been common thinking about the creative economy between London and Edinburgh, there has also been continuity in the broad institutional approaches taken, from the Lab-Lib coalition to the SNP.

Beyond the cultural ping-pong

Since coming to power, the SNP government's initiatives in cultural policy (and broadcasting) have been deeply influenced by current British thinking about the key role of the creative industries and the creative economy in conditions of global competition. The underlying ideas provide an ideological framework in Scotland, no less than in the UK as a whole, as outlined above. The Scottish approach to what culture means for the nation has not been identical to Westminster's. Rather, as with broadcasting, there have been occasional tensions between Scottish and UK-level policy rhetoric. This may be briefly illustrated by three set-piece speeches, delivered by the Scottish and UK Culture Secretaries while we were working on this book. The axis of argument, as may be expected, concerned how to balance cultural value and economic value.[49]

In April 2013, Maria Miller, then the UK Culture Secretary, spoke about fighting culture's corner in an age of austerity. Her speech emphasised the role that culture had to play in the UK's nascent economic recovery, seeing it as central to economic growth. Government spending had to be targeted, efficient, and see good returns – in short, culture had to offer good value for money. In June 2013, the Scottish Culture Secretary, Fiona Hyslop, responded directly to Miller's speech, focusing on how independence might positively impact on Scotland's culture and heritage sectors. In counterpoint, Hyslop stressed the intrinsic benefits of culture and creativity to the life of the nation.[50] Miller's next speech in January 2014 took a softer stance, emphasising how British culture was central to national identity and considered its intrinsic value.

Hyslop's address was undoubtedly a response to Miller in the fraught conditions of the independence campaign, when it made sense for her to emphasise the intrinsic worth of culture by distinguishing a Scottish from a British approach. However, Miller's January speech was a response to her critics south of the border rather than a direct address to her Scottish counterpart.

DOI: 10.1057/9781137478887.0005

Such speeches typify the repeated rhetorical tussle over what culture means to the life of the nation, where the debate over value for money typically intersects with ideas about the intrinsic worth of culture. But beyond such occasional rhetorical sallies, in Scotland, as in the rest of the UK, for the most part talk of culture routinely remains tightly bound up with the discourses of the creative economy and, in reality, policy imperatives are embedded in the institutional systems set up to underpin and develop this worldview. This has built on Scottish policy developments since 1999.

Joanne Orr has commented that 'culture was high on the agenda at the start of devolution, helping to shape a national identity with a wave of confidence and optimism'.[51] This was evident from a major Scottish Executive consultation in 1999, which sought to develop a national approach to culture.[52] The ensuing National Cultural Strategy resulted in an audit of Scottish cultural institutions and organisations. Two key policy shifts emerged in the wake of these reports. One major decision, effected in April 2007 by the Lab-Lib coalition in its dying days, was to move the national performing companies (Scottish Ballet, Scottish Opera, the Royal Scottish National Orchestra, the Scottish Chamber Orchestra and the National Theatre of Scotland) from being clients of the Scottish Arts Council to direct funding by the Scottish Government.[53] That arrangement has remained undisturbed by the change of party in power.

The other main policy decision was taken by the SNP when it came to power. That was to continue on their predecessors' path and to set up a new funding and development agency for the arts. This idea had come out of the National Cultural Strategy. It had been concluded that the Scottish Arts Council was no longer fit for purpose because of inefficiencies in the delivery of cultural services.[54] The Draft Culture Bill tabled in the Scottish Parliament by the Lab-Lib coalition proposed the dissolution of the Scottish Arts Council and the creation of a new funding and development agency that would 'not simply fund the arts, but also provide a stronger advocacy for cultural practitioners, providers and participants from across an expanded spectrum of cultural activity'.[55] While a focus on culture's contribution to the economy had been a mainstay of Scottish cultural policy since devolution, as may be seen from this move, ideas concerning the creative economy assumed particular importance from the mid-2000s.

In November 2007, the new SNP Government published its Economic Strategy, representing a shift in how the Scottish economy was managed and reported on. The purpose was '[t]o focus Government and public services on creating a more successful country, with opportunities for all of Scotland to flourish, through increasing sustainable economic growth.'[56] For those adopting a creative industries development strategy – as the Lab-Lib coalition did, and with which the SNP continued – having established a new focus or object for policy the task is to try and devise instruments to make it work better, in this case, to make more of a profitable business of culture. One of the consequences of this approach is to change the focus and functioning of public agencies operating in the public domain. This can involve renaming and reconstructing existing bodies or reorienting them profoundly by introducing new management styles. In Scotland, it was creative industries thinking that led directly to the establishment in 2010 of Creative Scotland.

Creative Scotland

The convoluted pre-history of Creative Scotland, the national agency for Scotland's arts, film and creative industries, remains to be told in full.[57] In outline, phase 1 was a long, uncertain gestation; phase 2 consisted of two attempts at making a 'transition'; and phase 3 consisted of the launch of Creative Scotland as a non-departmental public body (NDPB) on 1 July 2010, following the passage of the Public Services Reform (Scotland) Act. The setting-up of Creative Scotland entailed amalgamating the remits of two separate bodies, the Scottish Arts Council and Scottish Screen. The Scottish Arts Council was set up in 1994 following a restructuring of the Arts Council of Great Britain, but had worked autonomously under a Royal Charter since 1967. Scottish Screen was set up in 1997 to operate as the national development body for the screen industries. In the twilight zone between receiving their death sentences and being reborn as a single entity, these organisations shared a joint board. Both had been NDPBs, operating at arms' length from the government and were formally accountable to Scottish ministers.

Creative Scotland's structure was intended to innovate and was based in a critique of traditional arts council funding which was held to have created an unhelpful interdependency between arts officers and their clients. A novel relationship was conceived, mediated by a new-style officer, the portfolio manager, who would not 'own' a piece of cultural territory or work in a 'silo' and who could therefore evade capture by

DOI: 10.1057/9781137478887.0005

art-form interest groups. Creative Scotland was, then, conceived as a new prototype of the cultural agency: an investor rather than a funder, the leader of a number of partners sharing risks and finance. The blueprint for the organisation drew on the DCMS's ideas about the creative industries – clearly visible in the shift from 'art forms' to portfolios – as well as those of the innovation think-tank, NESTA. Prior to Creative Scotland's launch, the then Scottish Culture Minister, Mike Russell, recognised the tensions between entrepreneurial and cultural approaches but thought them to be reconcilable.[58]

However, such fundamental conflicts about cultural value cannot be wished away and discrepant viewpoints shaped by competing understandings fuelled the row that exploded in October 2012. An open letter, directed to Sir Sandy Crombie – Creative Scotland's inaugural Chairman – signed by a tally of more than 400 artists, accused the agency of 'ill-conceived decision-making; unclear language; lack of empathy and regard for Scottish culture' and much else besides. Questions of value were central to the artists' critique, with the open letter requesting that Creative Scotland 'revisit [its] policies with an eye to social and cultural as well as commercial value.'[59] Despite Creative Scotland's arms-length status as an NDPB, Scottish Culture Secretary Fiona Hyslop was forced to intervene when Crombie's response was deemed 'emollient' and 'patrician'[60] by one of the collective's de facto leaders, the playwright, David Greig; Hyslop requested Creative Scotland to attend to the artists' complaints as a matter of urgency. The controversy rumbled on throughout the autumn of 2012, and well into 2013. It eventually led to the resignation of Andrew Dixon, Creative Scotland's first CEO.

Such arguments between artists and agencies are not unusual; on this occasion, however, the impact of creative economy thinking on Creative Scotland's organisational architecture and its accompanying rhetoric may well have played a role in shaping the conflict.

Despite occupying a central position in the Scottish funding and support landscape, Creative Scotland is only one of a number of agencies that service the creative economy. As we have shown in this chapter, the development of the creative economy has entailed extensive intervention, and close management by governments at both UK and Scottish levels. The legacy of this, in the Scottish case in particular, is a quite complex funding and support landscape that creative business and practitioners must navigate.

DOI: 10.1057/9781137478887.0005

The creative consultant, Tom Fleming, basing his view on international research as well as that conducted across the UK, has noted the importance of 'highly specialised' intervention in the creative economy through 'dedicated intermediary and business support services (including advice), targeted training, export support and investment activities.'[61] However, how to intervene most effectively, he argues, means understanding questions of the scalability of businesses, their place in the value chain, and how rapidly transforming digital communications technologies are changing enterprises' positions in the market for given goods and services. From this perspective, the challenge for public bodies is to understand how best to construct the landscape of support and intervene effectively according to the type of business involved and the kind and levels of investment required.[62] In this regard, Scotland has floundered somewhat in recent years.[63]

Painting a new landscape?

Creative Scotland remains the major single distributor of government subsidy for artists and creative practitioners. It is also the lead partner in the Scottish Creative Industries Partnership (SCIP). The creation of this rather loose multi-agency grouping followed from a report by the cumbrously named Creative Industries Framework Agreement Implementation Group (CIFAIG). No small ambition lay behind that initiative: namely that 'Scotland becomes recognised as one of the world's most creative nations'.[64] SCIP was formed in 2009 and initially brought together the Convention of Scottish Local Authorities (COSLA), Highlands and Islands Enterprise (HIE), and Scottish Enterprise. All of these bodies signed a Framework Agreement. Launching the Agreement, the then Culture Minister Mike Russell stated: 'This agreement cements vital partnerships and ensures there is no wrong door for artists and creative practitioners seeking support. It ensures a seamless journey from the first point of contact.'[65] In fact the landscape was not as legible as the minister hoped. Nor was the journey for creatives to be as seamless as imagined.

In its initial incarnation SCIP brought together the two key enterprise agencies, the newly-minted Creative Scotland and local government, the latter being a major spender on culture and leisure. It embedded the DCMS's original categorisation of the 13 creative industry sectors in its thinking, while at the same time linking the framework to the Scottish Government's Economic Strategy, and in particular, the purpose of 'creating a more successful country, with opportunities for all of Scotland to flourish, through increasing sustainable economic growth.'[66]

SCIP was intended to promote 'joined-up' thinking in the creative sector, and to draw on the expertise embodied by a range of organisations, creative sector-specific and otherwise. Creative Scotland was also tasked with working with further bodies, such as the national skills agency, Skills Development Scotland (SDS), the Scottish Funding Council (which finances higher and further education), Business Gateway (which provides advice and support to enterprises) and the Sector Skills Councils. It was asked to ensure a continuous flow of research and information, the provision of advice, focused intervention, and regular stock taking by setting up a Creative Industries Coordination Group.[67] So far as 'accessing support' was concerned, the report identified CEO, the object of study of this book, as an agency contributing to that effort.

It was also hoped that SCIP would aid Scottish artists and creative practitioners in their navigation of the support and funding landscape.[68] 'In so far as possible', the report stated, 'organisations should share information and intelligence to avoid creative entrepreneurs having to repeat their information if they are referred onto another organisation. The role of Creative Scotland will be to collate, analyse and circulate the resulting information.'[69] Alongside creative sector-specific support organisations and coalitions, the new set-up was intended to ensure that creative businesses and practitioners might also qualify for funding and support from generic business support agencies such as Business Gateway, Scottish Enterprise, or Scottish Development International.

By 2014, the Framework established five years before was under review, with a view to improving the competence of creative companies. Skills Development Scotland led a review in order to develop a 'Skills Investment Plan for Creative Industries'. The Scottish Government sought to adapt the DCMS's creative industries thinking to local circumstance. Following its own redefinition, these now numbered 16 and broadly overlapped with the DCMS categories but also reflected the particular Scottish landscape.[70] According to Skills Development Scotland, the creative industries were a major contributor to the Scottish economy, accounting for 65,000 jobs, £2.7 billion in GVA and well over 12,000 businesses, of which 97 per cent were micro-enterprises.[71] Working with such micro-businesses – defined by the EC

DOI: 10.1057/9781137478887.0005

since 2005 as 'an enterprise which employs fewer than 10 persons and whose annual turnover and/or annual balance sheet does not exceed two million Euros' – has been precisely CEO's remit.[72] Software, writing and publishing, and advertising, design and architecture were identified as the largest sources of creative employment in Scotland. With a distinctly new emphasis, enterprise and skills agencies were envisaged as collaborating with higher and further education across the 'digital agenda', developing 'industry readiness and progression' and 'leadership and business skills' as well as 'new approaches to delivery'. Noting the rise in the number of graduates and undergraduates, a number of 'skills priorities' were identified, including those connected with digital innovation, entrepreneurship and leadership, and business and management. Once again, the desire to provide 'clear and comprehensive information on training, qualifications, creative roles & careers' was at the forefront as an objective. It cannot be doubted, therefore, that in Scottish creative industries policy, the economic dimension is foregrounded. When the review was being conducted in May 2014, it seemed likely that a new organisation would be set up: the Creative Industries Skills Partnership (CISP). Whether this will indeed be its designation and, if so, whether that would mean more than a different acronym for this grouping of agencies has yet to be seen.

Situating CEO

It will be obvious from the above account that a small support agency such as CEO fits first, into the broad sweep of UK creative industries policy, which has given a rationale to this type of cultural business support. And secondly, as we have seen, it is located in the specifically Scottish institutional variant of the British approach. This is the immediate context for understanding how CEO has had to position itself in practical terms, as a player in a crowded and quite complex scene. We shall explore this matter in much more detail in the chapters that follow.

But before we turn to the empirical detail, there is an analytical question to be considered. To what extent does the academic literature on the creative economy address the role of cultural business support? While one of the doyens of cultural policy research, the economist David Throsby, has observed that 'policy analysis should always pay attention to the institutional structures and administrative arrangements through

DOI: 10.1057/9781137478887.0005

which policy is delivered',[73] when it comes to cultural business support agencies, we have found that there has been precious little in-depth research. So far as we can ascertain, in its scope and certainly in its detail our study is unique, although others have researched cognate organisations. We therefore see this book as making a distinctive contribution to the developing study of cultural intermediaries.

Cultural intermediaries

Nearly four decades ago, in his magnum opus, *Distinction*, leading sociologist, Pierre Bourdieu, coined the term 'the new cultural intermediaries'. He was concerned, at least in part, with the emergence of new occupations in what would now be seen as the creative economy, and with part of what Richard Florida has termed the 'creative class'.[74]

Sean Nixon and Paul du Gay have suggested that 'there is serious need for more substantive work on cultural intermediary occupations in order to empirically ground claims about both their place in the occupational structure and the role they play in economic and cultural life'.[75] They point out that Bourdieu wanted 'to describe groups of workers involved in the provision of symbolic goods and services', identifying a range of media workers in this category as well as those, for instance, working in design, PR, marketing and advertising.

A body of work, influenced in part by Bourdieu, but also by new thinking in cultural economy, economic sociology and actor network theory, has built up in recent years. In a useful overview, Jennifer Smith Maguire and Julian Matthews have argued that we should pay attention to historical shifts in the structure of cultural intermediary occupations, focus on the kinds of practice and expert knowledge they use, and consider the impact that they have on tastes, values and markets.[76] The collection of studies they edited covers advertising, branding, public relations, arts promotion, fashion, popular music, lifestyle media and journalism, fitness, clothing, book retail and food and drink.

Their work does not cover research into cultural agencies conceived as intermediaries between a national policy system and everyday, small-scale cultural production. The more usual focus taken – as Keith Negus noted some years ago[77] – has been on the practices that intervene between cultural production and consumption. The term cultural intermediaries has tended to privilege those directly involved in 'symbolic mediation' as opposed to those that occupy supporting roles such as managers, business analysts and accountants. Liz McFall has pertinently suggested

DOI: 10.1057/9781137478887.0005

that the analysis of intermediaries should therefore include a 'diversity of forms [...] across a much broader range of actors than those concerned with making overtly symbolic interventions'.[78]

In effect, if not in its theoretical underpinnings, this rethinking converges with Greg Hearn and Ruth Bridgstock's view that 'there are as many, if not more, workers in creative cultural occupations employed outside creative industries firms than in creative industries firms'. This line reflects a current view among government statisticians and bodies such as NESTA.[79] Hearn and Bridgstock use the term 'embedded creatives' to designate this very broad category of worker. In their analysis, they distinguish between 'creative arts' and 'creative services' – it is the latter with which they are especially concerned, as 'a group of occupations that provide specialised creative expertise'.[80] Although they contend that 'cultural creative jobs are spread throughout all industrial sectors', the work of an agency that concerns itself solely with developing and using cultural business expertise does not specifically figure in their analysis.

Most pertinently, Justin O'Connor has suggested that cultural intermediaries in general have been changed by the policy shift from the cultural industries to the creative industries. He maintains that as the development of the cultural industries became increasingly widespread, it 'involved a much wider range of local cultural intermediaries than had previously been the case under art-centred policies'.[81] Among these he lists 'consultancies and policy advocates; arts administrators; cultural/ creative industry offices in an array of subsector development agencies; freelance project managers; urban planners and designers; and arts, cultural and 'creative agencies' in the public and private sectors and so on [...]'. However, while such intermediaries may first have developed in the cultural industries phase, the foregrounding of 'business development' and economic deliverables, argues O'Connor, is what has displaced earlier 'claims to social and cultural inclusion'.[82] O'Connor's analytical take was undoubtedly informed by his earlier empirical research into the workings of a cultural agency not unlike CEO.

This body, the Creative Industries Development Service (CIDS, which operated from 2000 to 2008) was set up in Manchester to act as an intermediary between local government and the creative sectors.[83] O'Connor and Gu have provided an analysis that is highly pertinent to the present work, and we shall discuss it further below. CIDS was gradually made redundant by shifts in the city council's strategy, not least the emphatic prioritisation of economics over culture, and the competition for

DOI: 10.1057/9781137478887.0005

resources by other agencies. CIDS found it hard to square the tensions that existed between the economic development focus of the local authority and the cultural discourse of the creative businesses it dealt with. As a not-for-profit body that worked in partnership with public agencies, CIDS shared some features with CEO. Its key rationale was to act as 'translator' between the 'dual languages of the creative sector and public policy'.[84] While it also set out to establish itself as a trusted spokesperson for creatives, at the same time, as a funder of projects it had to engage in what many involved in cultural work saw as the alienating practice of monitoring and evaluation. It was an organisation based on short-term funding and in that respect shared the precariousness of the creative sector, but at the same time, it was also comparatively better heeled. The tensions that led to its downfall are of less interest to us here than the fact that agencies such as CEO and CIDS do, evidently, encounter similar dilemmas that are inherently structured into the fields in which they operate.

It has taken quite some time for cultural analysts to focus strongly upon the kind of cultural intermediation analysed by O'Connor and Gu and us. If bodies such as CEO are one kind of typical creative economy intermediary, consultants are certainly another, and some have played an influential role in shaping the field, particularly at an early stage in its development. For instance, Charles Leadbeater and Kate Oakley's analysis, published in 1999, of what they called 'the independents', those they identified as 'Britain's new cultural entrepreneurs', set out many perspectives that are still largely in play. It was a typical product of the think-tank world of that moment.[85] This early intervention focused, albeit not in any depth, on 'cultural intermediaries and incubators', which they saw as key in helping 'cultural businesses with workspace, business advice and access to finance'.[86] This was an early insight into the focus of this book.[87]

Cultural entrepreneurs

Given its name, Cultural Enterprise Office is firmly located in the discourse of cultural entrepreneurship – which in the latest Scottish official discourse considered above has been renamed 'creative entrepreneurship'.[88] In their reflections on the various ways in which 'creative strategy' might be deployed, and thereby setting up a yardstick, Chris Bilton and Stephen Cummings have suggested that entrepreneurship works as 'the bridge between the art of innovation and a viable market'.[89] This perspective operates as a kind of regulative ideal that underlies the aspiration to make creatives more businesslike.

Revisiting the theme of cultural entrepreneurship, now from within academia, Kate Oakley has noted that this description often is used to characterise the 'self-employed cultural worker', where being entrepreneurial is regarded as 'encompassing aspects of self-employment, freelancing and portfolio working as well as the more "conscious" entrepreneurship of those who set up small businesses within the cultural sectors and seek to either work alone, or employ others as they grow'.[90] Entrepreneurship, often represented as a highly positive attribute in a capitalist society and economy, carries an important ideological charge in much official and popular discourse.[91] Oakley further notes that the contemporary idea of the cultural entrepreneur is 'difficult to separate either from the changes wrought by the growth of digital technology or from the idea of individualism'.[92] These are contingent conditions. Certainly, the idea of individual talent was embedded right at the heart of New Labour's framing of the creative industries. And, in the course of the best part of the intervening two decades, the 'digital economy' has become another major trope while, as noted, the disruptive effects of digitisation on the business models of major cultural industries – music, book publishing, newspapers, film-making, television programmes – have been at the centre of concern about copyright infringement.

Cultural entrepreneurship, Oakley rightly holds, is a contested idea and stronger in its rhetorical force than its analytical purchase. In this respect, it is similar to the idea of the creative economy itself. The idea of creativity has had huge appeal because it has a widespread ideological resonance: it accords with contemporary aspirations to seek self-realisation and fulfilment in work.[93] Certainly for some it has become intertwined with undertaking cultural enterprise. Although often officially presented as inclusive and democratic, creative economy policy is ultimately focused on a small minority's cultural labour and its successful commodification through the exercise of intellectual property rights – because that goes with the grain of how cultural markets actually work in a capitalist economy. As a system of beliefs, cultural entrepreneurship can provide orientation for the everyday conduct of creative workers in labour markets characterised by concentrations of power on the one hand and extreme precariousness on the other.[94]

The uncertainties of cultural enterprise were highlighted at the end of the nineties by Chris Bilton, notably the unpredictable value of what is

DOI: 10.1057/9781137478887.0005

produced, the delays between production and the realisation of a return, and the considerable weight of individual judgement in deciding what to produce.[95] He also noted, as have others, that the creative industries are mostly constituted by 'irregularly employed creative individuals' rather than 'more or less successful creative organisations with employees, assets and a regular financial turnover'. Bilton further observed that 'career paths and professional development in the creative industry [sic] follow a more meandering, less formal route than the training-to-employment model implies' and those best fitted to stay afloat maintain a portfolio career.[96]

When a business support agency treats sole traders and micro-businesses as cultural entrepreneurs that accords with an individualistic model of how to change behaviour. But at the same time, to offer support to creative work as a service also speaks to a wider, collective endeavour – legitimised, as we have seen, by the strivings of the competitive nation – and also depends on public intervention. Moreover, the individuals and micro-businesses addressed by the purveyors of business advice are often embedded in networks of mutual assistance in which non-monetary exchanges take place. In other words, intertwined with their individual strivings in the marketplace is their membership of a wider moral economy.[97] So we do need to temper the view that individualism totally rules all the value systems of the ostensible creative economy.

As an agency that engages with world of micro-businesses and sole traders, CEO may be conceived of as an intermediary between the policy framework established by the Scottish Government together with its lead agency, Creative Scotland, and the demand for business support services articulated by those directly engaged in creative work. It is in that precise sense that an agency such as CEO acts a curator of cultural enterprise. And, as we shall see, a particular curatorial theory and practice have been at the heart of CEO's business and its belief system. This has taken the form of endeavouring to identify the most appropriate 'journey' for its clients and imparting the skills and qualities needed to best fit them for survival and better in the creative economy.

Notes

1   Department for Culture, Media and Sport, *Creative industries economic estimates statistical release* (London: The Stationery Office, 2015), 4.

DOI: 10.1057/9781137478887.0005

2   For an exception, see this ironical take: John McDermott, 'Creative accounting by the boosters of creative industries', *Financial Times*, 14 January 2015: 6.

3   Department for Culture, Media and Sport, *Creative industries economic estimates*, 7.

4   Centre for Economic and Business Research, *The contribution of the arts and culture to the national economy* (London: CEBR, 2013), 2.

5   The Scottish Government, *Scotland's economy: the case for independence* (Edinburgh: The Scottish Government, 2013), 16.

6   As O'Brien notes, the economic focus has dominated the two other characteristic British preoccupations, cultural excellence and culture's community-building role, to become the present 'master narrative'. See Dave O'Brien, *Cultural policy: management, value and modernity in the creative industries* (London: Routledge, 2014), 41–46.

7   Andrew Gowers, *Gowers review of intellectual property* (London: The Stationery Office, 2006), 1.

8   *Ibid.*, 3.

9   Ian Hargreaves, *Digital opportunity: a review of intellectual property and growth* (London: Department for Business, Innovation and Skills, 2011), 3.

10   For some pertinent critiques see: Enrique Bustamante (ed.) *Industrias creativas: amenazas sobre la cultura digital* (Barcelona: Gedisa Editorial, 2011); Nicholas Garnham, 'From cultural to creative industries: an analysis of the implications of the "creative industries" approach to arts and media policymaking in the United Kingdom', *International Journal of Cultural Policy* 11 (2005); Justin O'Connor, *The cultural and creative industries: a literature review [2nd edition]* (London: Creativity, Culture and Education, 2010).

11   For useful surveys of the conceptual precursors of ideas about the creative economy, see: Mark Banks, *The politics of cultural work* (Basingstoke: Palgrave Macmillan, 2007); David Hesmondhalgh, *The cultural industries* (London: Sage, 2007); O'Connor, *The cultural and creative industries*. One road led from the Frankfurt School's critique of the 'culture industry' via the Marxist political economy of the 'cultural industries' to their recalibration as 'creative industries'.

12   Nicholas Garnham, *Capitalism and communication: global culture and the economics of information* (London: Sage, 1990), 154–168; Hesmondhalgh, *The cultural industries*.

13   Richard Florida, *The rise of the creative class, and how it's transforming work, leisure, community and everyday life* (New York: Basic Books, 2002); Jim McGuigan, *Cultural analysis* (London: Sage, 2010). A significant development of this kind has been MediaCityUK at Salford Quays in Greater Manchester, with the BBC North Group as its centre-piece. On Liverpool as European City of Culture, see Dave O'Brien, *Cultural policy*, 90–112.

DOI: 10.1057/9781137478887.0005

14   The socio-linguist, Norman Fairclough, has shown how 'assumptions about the global economy' led 'to an emphasis on competition between Britain and other countries [...] a project of "national renewal" designed to improve Britain's competitive position.' Norman Fairclough, *New Labour, new language?* (London: Routledge, 2000), 22–23.

15   Department for Culture, Media and Sport, *Creative industries mapping document* (London: The Stationery Office, 1998), 3.

16   Ibid.

17   Garnham, 'From cultural to creative industries,' 15–16. In today's parlance, we would be talking about the digital economy as at the heart of the creative economy.

18   See: United Nations Conference on Trade and Development, *Creative economy report 2008* (Geneva: UNCTAD, 2008), and subsequent reports; The Work Foundation, *Staying ahead: the economic performance of the UK's creative industries* (London: The Work Foundation, 2007).

19   McGuigan, *Cultural analysis*, 117–129.

20   David Harvey, *A brief history of neoliberalism* (Oxford: Oxford University Press, 2005), 2.

21   David Hesmondhalgh, Melissa Nisbett, Kate Oakley and David Lee, 'Were New Labour's cultural policies neo-liberal?' *International Journal of Cultural Policy* 21 (2015): 13.

22   At this time of writing, just before the UK General Election of May 2015, it is impossible to say which policies will be pursued next at Westminster and in Whitehall, although the likelihood of significant change is small.

23   For analyses of New Labour discourse and of the policy thinktankerati, see: Philip Schlesinger, 'Creativity: from discourse to doctrine?' *Screen* 48 (2007); Schlesinger, 'Creativity and the experts: New Labour, think tanks, and the policy process'. *The International Journal of Press/Politics* 14 (2009): 3–20. For an overview of the literature, see O'Connor, *The cultural and creative industries.*

24   John Howkins, *The creative economy: how people make money from ideas* (London: Penguin, 2001). Howkins considers 15 'core creative industries', as compared to the DCMS's 13.

25   Ibid., 79.

26   Ibid., 211.

27   'Creative Europe', European Commission, accessed 3 March 2015, http://ec.europa.eu/programmes/creative-europe/index_en.htm.

28   'KEA selected to advise on the improvement of culture and creative sectors' statistics in the EU', KEA, accessed 3 March 2015, http://www.keanet.eu/. The figures cited are contained in this communiqué, as are details of the 'high-level experts' advising on the data collection, including the UK innovation think-tank, NESTA.

DOI: 10.1057/9781137478887.0005

29 UNCTAD, *Creative economy report*, 3.

30 Ibid., 5.

31 Ibid., 143.

32 Terry Flew, *The creative industries: culture and policy* (London: Sage, 2012).

33 Stuart Cunningham, *Hidden innovation: policy, industry and the creative sector* (Lanham, MN: Lexington Books, 2014).

34 Gillian Doyle, Philip Schlesinger, Raymond Boyle and Lisa W. Kelly, *The rise and fall of the UK Film Council* (Edinburgh: Edinburgh University Press, 2015).

35 Cited in Kate Oakley, David Hesmondhalgh, David Lee and Melissa Nisbett, 'The national trust for talent? NESTA and New Labour's cultural policy', *British Politics* 9 (2014): 305.

36 Ibid., 297.

37 Ibid., 302–303.

38 Ibid., 310.

39 Ibid., 311.

40 Neil MacCormick, *Questioning sovereignty: law, state and nation in the European Commonwealth* (Oxford: Oxford University Press, 1999); David McCrone, *The sociology of nationalism* (London: Routledge, 1998).

41 The Smith Commission, *Smith Commission report* (Edinburgh: The Smith Commission, 2014), accessed 9 March 2015, http://www.smith-commission. scot/wp-content/uploads/2014/11/The_Smith_Commission_Report-1.pdf.

42 At this time of writing, the outcome remains unresolved and politically contentious, with the full legislative process and parliamentary debate to follow the May 2015 General Election.

43 The Scottish Government, *Scotland's future* (Edinburgh: The Scottish Government, 2013), 96–123.

44 NESTA, *The geography of the UK's creative and high-tech economies* (London: NESTA, 2015), 4–5.

45 Philip Schlesinger, 'The SNP, cultural policy and the idea of the "creative economy"', in *The modern SNP: from protest to power*, ed. Gerry Hassan (Edinburgh: Edinburgh University Press, 2009), 135–146.

46 The Smith Commission, *The Smith Commission report*, 17.

47 Lindsay Paterson, *The autonomy of modern Scotland* (Edinburgh: Edinburgh University Press, 1994); Lindsay Paterson, 'Utopian pragmatism: Scotland's choice', *Scottish Affairs*, 24 (2015): 22–46.

48 Michael Billig, *Banal nationalism* (London: Sage, 1995).

49 For a recent review of the British debate that seeks to burnish the concept of 'cultural ecology' 'congruent with cultural value approaches that take into account a wide range of non-monetary values', see John Holden, *The ecology of culture: a report commissioned by the Arts and Humanities Research Council's Cultural Value project* (Swindon: Arts and Humanities Research Council, 2015), 3.

DOI: 10.1057/9781137478887.0005

50 This was a new departure for the Scottish Government, for whom the creative industries have been integral to their National Performance Indicators.

51 Joanne Orr, 'Instrumental or intrinsic? Cultural policy in Scotland after devolution', *Cultural Trends* 17 (2008), 310.

52 This was the name of Scotland's administration before the SNP changed it to the Scottish Government.

53 Susan Galloway and Huw Jones, 'The Scottish dimension of British arts government: a historical perspective', *Cultural Trends* 19 (2010).

54 Ibid., 33–35.

55 David Stevenson, 'Tartan and tantrums: critical reflections on the Creative Scotland "stooshie"', *Cultural Trends* 23 (2014).

56 The Scottish Government, *Economic strategy* (Edinburgh: The Scottish Government, 2007), vii.

57 Galloway and Jones 'The Scottish dimension'; Orr, 'Instrumental or intrinsic?'; Stevenson 'Tartans and tantrums'.

58 Schlesinger, 'The SNP, cultural policy and the idea of the "creative economy"', 143.

59 'Open letter to Creative Scotland', Sam Ainsley et al., accessed 9 March 2015, http://www.bbc.co.uk/news/uk-scotland-19880680.

60 Brian Ferguson, 'Creative Scotland must be "pulled apart" say campaigners', *The Scotsman*, 11 October 2012, accessed 9 March 2015. http://www.scotsman.com/lifestyle/arts/news/creative-scotland-must-be-pulled-apart-say-campaigners-1-2567606.

61 Tom Fleming, 'Investment and funding for creative enterprises in the UK', in *Entrepreneurship in the creative industries: an international perspective*, ed. Colette Henry (Cheltenham: Edward Elgar, 2007), 107–125.

62 Ibid., 117.

63 Fleming had a role in the consultations that eventually led to the creation of Creative Scotland. In 2008, he and John Knell were commissioned by the Creative Scotland Transition Project to map the creative industries in Scotland and outline strategies for future growth. Subsequently, in 2013, Fleming was commissioned to develop a strategy for Creative Scotland's creative industries support. Delivered late in 2014, at this time of writing the report has not so far seen the light of day.

64 The Scottish Government, *Scotland's creative industries partnership report* (Edinburgh: Scottish Government, 2009), 1.

65 'Support for creative industries', The Scottish Government, accessed 9 March 2015, http://scotland.gov.uk/News/Releases/2009/06/18132606.

66 The Scottish Government, *Scotland's creative industries partnership report*, 2.

67 Ibid., 3–4.

68 At this time of writing, SCIP's functioning is under review.

69 Ibid., 6.

DOI: 10.1057/9781137478887.0005

70 They are: advertising; architecture; cultural education; computer games; crafts and antiques; design; fashion and textiles; film and video; libraries and archives; music; performing arts; photography; software and electronic publishing; TV and radio; visual arts; writing and publishing. Compare the original DCMS categories listed above.

71 The account that follows is taken with permission from: David Martin and Mili Shukla, 'Skills Investment Plan for creative industries' (presentation made to the Joint Skills Committee, 8 May 2014). The data presented by Martin and Shukla drew on a study commissioned by Creative Scotland and Scottish Enterprise from DC Research: DC Research, *Economic contribution study: an approach to the economic assessment of arts & creative industries in Scotland* (Carlisle: DC Research, 2012).

72 European Commission, *The new SME definition: user guide and model declaration* (Brussels: European Commission, 2005), 15.

73 David Throsby, 'A new "moment" for cultural policy?' In *Making meaning, making money: directions for the arts and cultural industries in the creative age*, ed. Lisa Andersen and Kate Oakley (Newcastle upon Tyne: Cambridge Scholars Publishing, 2008), 13.

74 Pierre Bourdieu, *Distinction: a social critique of the judgement of taste* (London: Routledge and Kegan Paul, 1984), 326–327; Richard Florida, *The rise of the creative class*. We shall not comment here on the great theoretical and political distance between these two projects.

75 Sean Nixon and Paul du Gay, 'Who needs cultural intermediaries?', 498.

76 Jennifer Smith Maguire and Julian Matthews, 'Introduction', in *The cultural intermediaries reader*, ed. Jennifer Smith Maguire and Julian Matthews (London: Sage, 2014), 8–11.

77 Keith Negus, 'The work of cultural intermediaries'.

78 Liz McFall, 'Problems in the economy of qualities', in Maguire and Matthews, *The cultural intermediaries reader*, 51. For reasons of space, we cannot engage with the wider issues raised here.

79 NESTA, *A manifesto for the creative economy* (London: NESTA, 2013); Department for Culture, Media and Sport, *Creative industries economic estimates*.

80 Greg Hearn and Ruth Bridgstock, 'The curious case of the embedded creative: creative cultural occupations outside the creative industries', in *Handbook of management and creativity*, ed. Chris Bilton and Stephen Cummings (Cheltenham: Edward Elgar, 2014); Cunningham, *Hidden innovation*, 199–149.

81 O'Connor, 'Intermediaries and imaginaries', 7.

82 Ibid., 8.

83 O'Connor and Gu, 'Developing a creative cluster'.

84 Ibid., 131.

85 Schlesinger, 'Creativity and the experts'.

DOI: 10.1057/9781137478887.0005

86　Charles Leadbeater and Kate Oakley, *The independents: Britain's new cultural entrepreneurs* (London: Demos, 1999), 44.

87　It is much more common to read consultants' output than their own reflections on their job. For some insights, see Russell Prince, 'Consultants and the global assemblage of culture and creativity', *Transactions of the Institute of British Geographers*, 39 (2014).

88　Scottish Government, *Growth, talent, ambition: the Government's strategy for the creative industries* (Edinburgh: Scottish Government, 2011).

89　Chris Bilton and Stephen Cummings, *Creative strategy: reconnecting business and innovation* (Chichester: Wiley, 2010), 107.

90　Kate Oakley, 'Good work? Rethinking cultural entrepreneurship', in *Handbook of management and creativity*, ed. Chris Bilton and Stephen Cummings (Cheltenham: Edward Elgar, 2014), 145.

91　Raymond Boyle and Lisa Kelly, *The television entrepreneurs* (Farnham: Ashgate, 2012), 7–25.

92　Oakley, 'Good work?', 146.

93　Luc Boltanski and Eve Chiapello, *The new spirit of capitalism* (London: Verso, 2007).

94　David Hesmondhalgh and Sarah Baker, *Creative labour: media work in three cultural industries* (London: Routledge, 2011); Pierre-Michel Menger, *Le travail créateur: s'accomplir dans l'incertain* (Paris: Seuil/Gallimard, 2009); Gerald Raunig, Gene Ray and Ulf Wuggenig, eds, *Critique of creativity: precarity, subjectivity and resistance in the 'creative industries'* (London: Mayfly Books, 2011).

95　Chris Bilton, 'Risky business', *Cultural Policy* 6 (1999): 19–20.

96　Ibid., 28–29.

97　Banks, *The politics of cultural work*; Holden, *The ecology of culture*.

DOI: 10.1057/9781137478887.0005

3
Origins and Development of CEO

Abstract: *This chapter outlines the evolution of Cultural Enterprise Office over 15 years, tracing its development from the initial feasibility study in 1999, through its launch and four phases of operation. The final section sets out the shape of the organisation and its main business support activities during the period of observation (2013–2014). The chapter addresses the role of institutional narrative; CEO's changing geographic remit; the way the organisation has drawn on and modified operational models from elsewhere; how it has intersected with and adapted itself to the existing local and national business support infrastructure. It concludes that the quest for survival has required CEO to continually adapt, re-orientating itself towards different sources of funding and responding to current policy trends.*

Keywords: business support; incubators; NESTA; organisational narratives; Scottish policy

Schlesinger, Philip, Melanie Selfe and Ealasaid Munro. *Curators of Cultural Enterprise: A Critical Analysis of a Creative Business Intermediary*. Basingstoke: Palgrave Macmillan, 2015. DOI: 10.1057/9781137478887.0006.

DOI: 10.1057/9781137478887.0006

Despite its lack of a consistent stream of core funding, CEO has operated continuously in a precarious sector for 13 years. In this time, various other cultural support organisations have fallen by the wayside. Consequently, one of the goals of this book is to understand how CEO has survived and developed over time. The sketch history of CEO presented here has been conceived with an eye to two interconnected questions. First, how has the organisation managed to make and remake a place for itself within a shifting policy landscape? Second, where do CEO's ideas, practices and values come from and how have they evolved over time? In this chapter, we map the forces that led to its creation as well as the routine working practices we encountered when we entered the field. In Chapters 4 and 5, CEO's value systems, continuing challenges and forward strategy will be explored in greater depth.

The wider context for CEO's development lies in the growth of creative industries and creative economy thinking at the UK and Scottish levels outlined in the previous chapter. Here, we concentrate on the case of a single historically and geographical situated agency. This permits us to show how quite general concepts embodied in British policy discourse are applied in practice, in relation to a specific local and national agenda in Scotland. As O'Connor and Gu note, ' "creative industries," though often defined in the placeless language of the "knowledge economy," "creativity," and "innovation," are rooted in and held to exemplify complex local histories and cultures'.[1] Therefore, we trace CEO's development from an initial, limited, perception of a need to provide specialist business skills support for emerging artists in Glasgow in the late 1990s to its current incarnation as a body with ambitions on a broader scale. In its present form, CEO seeks to deliver business knowhow, Scotland-wide, to a range of creative sector micro-businesses and sole traders at different stages of their professional and business development. In particular, we wish to demonstrate how three interrelated factors have been crucial to creating the version of CEO in operation as we write: the way the organisation has drawn on and modified operational models from elsewhere; how it has intersected with and adapted to the existing local and national business support infrastructure; and how its quest for survival has required CEO to re-orientate itself continually towards different sources of funding and align itself with different policy agendas at key moments.

DOI: 10.1057/9781137478887.0006

Funding, phases and organisational narrative

Narratives told within CEO offer an important key to its organisational history. Perhaps unsurprisingly for an organisation that expanded from a team of three in 2002 to 19 employees during the period in which our study was undertaken, staff knowledge of the background that had shaped CEO's ethos and working practices was uneven. Nevertheless, there was a clear sense of shared organisational values and of the centrality of change, the latter reflecting both the fact that CEO had been through a number of different operational phases and an acute organisation-wide awareness of CEO's precariousness in relation to its funding. While this knowledge was felt and expressed diversely depending on staff members' role and length of service, collectively it has shaped the way the organisation understands its own survival and its relationship to its client base. Crucially, our early discussions regarding the possibility of conducting this study revealed that for the Director, Deborah Keogh, a major motivation for letting us into CEO was the hope that it would help to produce a 'new narrative' about the organisation and the meaning of its work to its clients. This wish derived from the combination of a pragmatic need to make a convincing policy case for continued support, along with a deep frustration. CEO's leadership did not think that the dominant economically-focused metrics for measuring both business success and the effects of intervention were able to represent what they perceived as the true value both of their agency and the creative micro-businesses it was serving.

Indeed, particularly for Keogh, the practical aspects of the constant quest for funding strongly shaped both her personal sense of CEO's development, and the way she communicated this within and beyond CEO. Her sense of taking the organisation through distinct operational phases was punctuated by key moments in the cycle of seeking and obtaining funding packages and delivering on the related objectives. The process of putting together successive funding applications, in combination with the more informal pitching and personal persuasion required to convince potential funders to support CEO, meant that Keogh repeatedly needed to articulate and re-orientate the organisational narrative for different audiences. While these versions of CEO's history and purpose were cumulative – the most-recently written account providing a basis for the next – they were also tailored. Each account highlighted the most successful and locally useful features of an organisational history for the

DOI: 10.1057/9781137478887.0006

policy moment and task in hand, resulting on every occasion in a highly instrumental and future-focused backwards glance. By necessity, these were upbeat iterations, which tended to emphasise CEO as proactive, moving forward decisively in response to perceived needs and opportunities. However, the imperative to present CEO as a bounded entity and foreground its innovation, activity and pertinence inevitably worked to minimise a number of other narrative elements: the degree to which CEO was both connected to and influenced by a wider field of support practice; the ways in which individuals, ideas and models of practice have moved into and out of the organisation; and also what was learned and retained from failed or problematic enterprises. These kinds of knowledge, we found, have had a shadowy existence within the organisation, emerging as partial narratives in interviews, casual conversations and through our observations of organisational discourse, in conjunction with the traces found in routine organisational documentation.

While official project dates and reporting schedules might seem to offer neat boundaries between the different phases of CEO's operation, in practice they are imprecise; each operational phase has had a significant gestation period and has left a legacy of practice in its wake, only some of which is visible or recognised as such within the organisation. In interviews, Keogh and other members of the senior management team displayed a fluid, overlapping sense of the temporality of CEO's operational phases, as the roots of each period of operation were inevitably to be found in the preceding one. Similarly, as we came to know the organisation better and asked more specific questions, many of the practices and terms that initially puzzled us turned out to be remnants of earlier phases and their logics. In outlining the four key phases of CEO's life to date, we have used dates that represent broad shifts in organisational aims and thinking. Our purpose is to highlight some key themes, patterns and tensions derived from the combined analysis of our interviews, observation and documentation.

Beginnings, 1999–2004

CEO began life in November 2001 as the Cultural Enterprise Unit.[2] This was a three-year, pilot project with a staff of three and a drop-in office that opened in May 2002 in the newly refurbished Centre for Contemporary Arts (CCA) on Sauchiehall Street in Glasgow's city centre. The funding

DOI: 10.1057/9781137478887.0006

came mostly from the European Regional Development Fund and Scottish Enterprise Glasgow, with smaller but significant support also coming from the Scottish Arts Council and Glasgow City Council.

The impetus for the project came from Scottish Enterprise Glasgow and the Scottish Arts Council, which in conjunction with the proposed host venue, CCA, and the British Council International Cultural Desk, commissioned a feasibility study conducted by an existing cultural business support body, Cultural Enterprise Cardiff in January 1999.[3] This focus on the creative sector reflected the wider New Labour policy drive, already outlined, to position the creative industries as economically vital and valuable. At a Scottish level, the creative and cultural industries had been identified as having the potential for rapid growth. In Glasgow, which had been designated European City of Culture in 1990, particular attention focused on the regenerative potential of culture within the city. However, in 1998 the Glasgow Cultural Statistics Framework[4] had highlighted signs of a local downturn, and this was used to make the case for developing specialist business support designed to help Glasgow consolidate its post-1990 City of Culture status as a centre for creativity and cultural production.

A key aspect of creative economy policy and its implementation is the way that particular modes of support emerge and are replicated across the sector. One mechanism by which models of practice and the underlying values they embody are circulated is through the work of those who combine service delivery and consultancy. Frequently, versions of an established delivery model are propagated by undertaking consultancy and reaching the obvious conclusion that something fit for purpose already exists. Cultural Enterprise Cardiff (1995–2007) was an independent, not-for-profit company (a status CEO eventually attained in 2009) and, in addition to the nearly identical name, was a precursor to how CEO ultimately developed in Glasgow. The Cardiff model consisted of an information service, one-to-one advice sessions, a network of creative and specialist business knowledge mentors and a consultancy, with the latter designed to be financially self-sustaining. The feasibility study, authored by what was then the organisation's consultancy arm, David Clarke Associates Ltd (DCA Ltd), recommended the same combination for Glasgow.[5]

When we compare the early development of Cultural Enterprise Cardiff and CEO, it is clear there were many similarities, not just in aims and support activities but also in strategy and process. Although the

DOI: 10.1057/9781137478887.0006

Cardiff organisation was set up without a prior consultancy occurring, the mix of local partners involved and the pattern of seeking funds to establish and develop the organisation strongly prefigured CEO. As with Glasgow, there was a host arts organisation that would ultimately become the venue, working in Cardiff with a pair of mainstream business support agencies.[6] Having identified a gap in provision for the sector, they used a small, local investment to pilot the project and put together a bid for three-year funding under the European Regional Development Fund. Cultural Enterprise Cardiff also established the model of expansion that Glasgow would ultimately follow, initially serving the city before extending its services to businesses from anywhere in Wales during the second funded phase. However, in the case of Cultural Enterprise Cardiff, it was notable that the Arts Council of Wales was not initially party to the plan, but was only 'later persuaded of the value of enterprise support' and by 2000 was contributing through 'grant in aid and lottery funds.'[7] By contrast, the involvement in Glasgow of the Scottish Arts Council from the outset suggests that the concept of enterprise support had been more readily accepted by official Scottish arts policy thinking between 1995 and 1999.

The focus on micro-businesses and sole traders was shared by both the Cardiff and Glasgow Cultural Enterprise projects, although there were small but significant differences in the definition of potential clients, which was largely a consequence of the specificity of the existing Scottish business support landscape. One striking feature of CEO's initial remit – to support 'sole arts practitioners and cultural micro-business' – was not only its focus on the small scale but also a concentration on arts practitioners rather than the more commercially-orientated creative industries.[8] Moreover, unlike Cultural Enterprise Cardiff, which offered support across all career stages, it was aimed exclusively at those at a very early stage of career development. This restricted remit was designed to ensure distinctiveness in support without creating an overlap in provision. CEO was positioned as addressing a highly specific perceived gap in support: between those graduating from university in a creative field and their eventually finding or making a place within the sector. CEO's initial role was to ensure that creative practitioners at the 'pre-entry' level became 'business ready' by developing entrepreneurial skills at the business idea stage.

For Scottish Enterprise Glasgow, as the main Scottish funder and lead agency for the European Regional Development Fund applications,

DOI: 10.1057/9781137478887.0006

CEO was a small part of a complex business support landscape, and the new organisation's successful integration with the mainstream support agency, Business Gateway, was seen as of central importance by its funders. In addition to providing 'bespoke' advice directly to creative practitioners, a secondary CEO objective was to improve the quality of creative business support across the support landscape by attuning Business Gateway 'to issues specific to the cultural & creative sector'.[9] Consequently, management of the CEO project was contracted out to the local Business Gateway service provider, Glasgow Opportunities. However, as support agencies are routinely evaluated in terms of the number of 'assists' they provide, it was not initially appropriate for CEO to tread on the toes of the generalist agencies by seeking to provide direct support to more established creative businesses, however micro in scale. As the new entrant in the field, CEO's own footprint needed to be small and precisely placed, slotting into the space left by existing provision.

During the first three years of operation the 'core' services offered by CEO were established. As the restrictive early-stage remit precluded its having the business consultancy element that DCA Ltd had recommended, CEO's initial focus was on providing one-to-one advice 'surgeries' and building a specialist business information service incorporating online resources, telephone support and referrals to other relevant support bodies. To this they added a coaching service, which was a more appropriate third string for supporting early stage creative practitioners. However, as some of the external courses on offer from organisations such as Business Gateway seemed inappropriately pitched for creative clients, over the course of 2002–2003 CEO began to draw on freelance staff to develop and deliver a sector-specific series of business skills training workshops. It also started to develop relationships with external bodies, delivering training through higher education institutions and professional organisations. While clearly focused on the identified skills gap, this represented a significant expansion of the original project and enabled CEO to reach many more clients,[10] as well as start to build a stream of additional income. Information, advice and training events have remained the core CEO services, and as Chapter 4 will explore, coaching has remained central to the CEO approach, marking these early developments as the foundations on which the organisation was built.

A number of central principles regarding how clients should be valued, respected and supported can also be traced back to the feasibility

DOI: 10.1057/9781137478887.0006

study. One recommendation was that CEO should *not* itself award funds, as this would compromise its ability to offer the best support and advice to all clients as they navigated funding and support opportunities. Underpinning the non-funding approach lay another more fundamental principle, which has remained central to CEO's advisory ethos: a commitment to refrain from any critique of the artistic merits of the work, instead focusing solely on the business plan. In combination, these rules set CEO apart from the critical evaluations of relative artistic merit inherent in the work of grant-awarding bodies such as the Scottish Arts Council and its successor, Creative Scotland.

Four Cities, 2004–2009

In 2004, following a positive interim report on the first phase,[11] CEO secured three years of European funding, totalling £995,000, to roll out its services to major Scottish cities other than Glasgow. This was conceived as the first stage towards delivering a truly national Scottish service,[12] and meant a narrative reframing of the first phase, now placing less emphasis on CEO's Glasgow-specific relevance and more on the value of Glasgow as providing a single-city pilot for a service aiming at achieving national reach and profile. However, the sprawling and unevenly populated geography of Scotland, coupled with the diverse composition and distribution of the creative sectors in and around each city node, made rolling out a nationwide service more complex in practice than on paper.

The largest portion of the funding (£412,000) came from European Structural Funds, designed to provide 'Member States and regions with assistance to overcome structural deficiencies and to enable them to strengthen competitiveness and increase employment'.[13] However, there was also a range of other stakeholders contributing to the financing and thus the shape and governance of the project. Scottish Enterprise National contributed £278,000. A further £150,000 came from the Scottish Arts Council, and smaller amounts from Glasgow (£60,000), Dundee (£25,000) and Aberdeen (£25,000) city councils respectively. The 2006 evaluation report highlighted Edinburgh City Council as a notable omission from the funding mix, with a smaller contribution from Edinburgh College of Art (£22,000) covering a more limited range of provision in the capital.[14] While Edinburgh City Council did eventually

DOI: 10.1057/9781137478887.0006

come onboard, this process highlights the difficulty of simultaneously managing many small contributor stakeholders.

As a strategic shift, the aim to reach beyond metropolitan centres was in tune with wider policy thinking, which was increasingly turning to regional and rural development. However, it was only a partial success. In addition to the difficulty of securing equitable funding from all the city councils, delivering an evenly distributed service proved impossible. A hub-and-spoke model was adopted, with Glasgow functioning as headquarters, supporting three part-time offices located within established arts spaces in Edinburgh, Dundee and Aberdeen. However, CEO's client base remained overwhelmingly concentrated in the more densely populated central belt.[15] Aberdeen emerged as a particularly difficult area to serve, as many Aberdeen-based events were hard to mount. Part of the challenge was that while the contributing stakeholder was Aberdeen city council, the local creative community was less of an urban cluster than a rural scatter, dispersed across a large shire, and thus potential clients still faced significant journeys to attend their 'local' CEO events.

In 2007–2008, two unsuccessful European Regional Development Fund bids were made, one to continue to serve the Lowlands and Uplands and another to expand the service to the Highlands and Islands. The difficulties experienced in Aberdeen indicate that the challenges of delivering CEO services further afield on roughly the same model as in more urban concentrations might have been insurmountable. However, the failure to secure either award was perhaps more to do with the shifting priorities of the funder. CEO's commitment to delivering business support to an already highly-qualified client base in a demand-driven way was at odds with the European Regional Development Fund's recently redefined emphasis on improving employment opportunities for those in disadvantaged demographic groups and its new focus on developing the regional and rural skills base through formal accreditation and qualifications.

Although CEO's primary emphasis was still on the pre-start-up business phase, in practice, it was beginning to expand to cover established businesses too. It was also at this stage that CEO began to frame itself with growing explicitness as a self-defined 'translation' service – as specialists in converting business knowhow into the right register to appeal to the creative sector.

This second phase also saw CEO expand the breadth and reach of its core services in other ways. Professional Development Planning (PDP)

DOI: 10.1057/9781137478887.0006

sessions expressly extended the offer beyond the initial focus on early-stage businesses, taking a more creative career-centred approach and inviting those at any stage to take stock and plan their long-term goals and next moves. More partnership working was also added to the core advice and information service mix. CEO engaged in more specialist projects, such as the 12-month Artist as Leader research programme, in conjunction with Robert Gordon University and Performing Arts Labs in 2006–2007.[16]

By September 2008, when CEO's office moved to new premises on Bell Street, on the edge of the city's creative district, regional advisers were based in Glasgow, Aberdeen, Dundee and Edinburgh and a range of specialist advisers covering creative sector and business specialisms were now employed on a freelance basis.

New projects, 2009–2012

While the loss of European Regional Development Fund support was a disappointment, the Scottish Government filled the gap. Its willingness to step in may have been in part due to the uncertain course of cultural policy at the time. As explored in Chapter 2, in 2008, the Scottish Arts Council and Scottish Screen began their lengthy and controversial path towards merger, becoming Creative Scotland in 2010. In this context, although small, a body such as CEO could provide a degree of continuity of support for the sector.

This phase also saw a significant evolution in the shape and governance of CEO. In late 2009, CEO became an independent agency. This marked a key point in CEO's development: initially it had operated as a series of discrete projects, but now it began to reframe itself more explicitly as an organisation, delivering a more diverse range of projects on various timescales. It also now answered to a Board rather than a steering committee.

There was still considerable continuity in day-to-day delivery. Although it ceased to have an Aberdeen-based adviser in 2011, between 2009 and 2012 CEO still largely retained the Four City shape of its core service established during the previous phase of operation. CEO's trading arm continued to develop events in partnership with external bodies, and most significantly, in 2009 CEO took on sole responsibility for the NESTA-originated Starter for 6, delivering its first full cycle in 2010.

DOI: 10.1057/9781137478887.0006

This became CEO's first major recurring programme, and brought with it a substantial budget and an increased public profile. However, as it involved awarding money within a competitive framework, it also introduced a potential conflict with the established CEO ethos of providing support without making a judgement of the work, making this founding principle increasingly difficult to sustain in practice.

Starter for 6 grew out of the Creative Pioneer Programme, developed and run by NESTA in the early 2000s. Its inaugural run in 2003 came just as New Labour was in the process of positioning the creative industries as a high growth sector. The Creative Pioneer Programme was developed by an ex-CEO employee, Siân Prime. She was later called upon to pare it down for development into Starter for 6.

NESTA piloted Starter for 6 in 2006, as a streamlined alternative to the Creative Pioneer Programme. As with many of NESTA's other programmes, the idea was to pass on Starter for 6 to other bodies after it had been piloted and evaluated. CEO was heavily involved in the process. In its original NESTA incarnation, Starter for 6 drew heavily on CEO's pool of regional and specialist advisers. Therefore, as a result of its prior involvement in the development phase, CEO was the only contender to take on the programme after it had been evaluated.

The handover from NESTA to CEO happened very rapidly, with only two weeks between the programme coming in-house and being launched. Lynsey Smith had helped to pilot the programme at NESTA before moving to CEO. She oversaw Starter for 6's inaugural year there, but left shortly after. At CEO, Starter for 6 needed to be reshaped, shifting from NESTA's general focus on innovation towards the creative industries. Starter for 6 began to redefine CEO, engendering a greater emphasis on design- and technology-focused businesses than the original artist or maker client base.

The quest for stability, 2012 onwards

In May 2012, CEO relocated from Bell Street to new premises in South Block on Osborne Street. Although only a short distance away, this move firmly repositioned the organisation in the heartlands of Glasgow's main creative district, on the second floor of a building housing a range of other creative businesses. South Block is a development initiated and run by WASPS,[17] a non-profit company and charity providing affordable

DOI: 10.1057/9781137478887.0006

studio space for artists and arts organisations at 17 sites around Scotland. Thus, the move brought CEO physically closer to some of its client base.[18] This was also the point at which we, as a research team, came into the picture, with one of the key meetings planning the shape of the proposed research coinciding with the week of the office relocation. Our experience of being caught up within the process of change therefore affected the way we sought to understand the organisation and its work.

As will be discussed later, the organisation underwent an internal restructuring during the period of observation, designed to devolve certain aspects of decision-making as part of a wider future-proofing strategy. In order to provide a framework for the analysis that follows in Chapters 4 and 5, we next set out a baseline account of CEO's working practices, outlining the range of CEO's work at the time of our research and highlighting how the operation has been shaped by its earlier phases.

The shape of CEO services

CEO's incremental evolution has resulted in shifts in how the organisation has thought about different aspects of its work, the relationships between these and, as the agency has expanded, the demarcation of roles and responsibilities between teams and individual staff. During our interviews and observation, CEO's management repeatedly made administrative, budgetary and conceptual distinctions between services that were 'core' and those that were not, usually termed 'projects' (normally one-off and time-limited and often delivered in partnership with other organisations) or, increasingly, called 'programmes' (regular or recurring schemes). Chapter 4 will focus on the relationship between the different values embedded in the core and programme aspects of the service, but in the remainder of this chapter, the aim is to set out how these combined in routine administration and working practice.

Core activities

The core service elements (information, advice and events) have been delivered by two overlapping staff teams, drawing on a spectrum of freelance specialist advisers. The largest staff team is Business Support, which during the period of observation consisted of a manager, together with three frontline office staff who fielded phone and email enquiries and

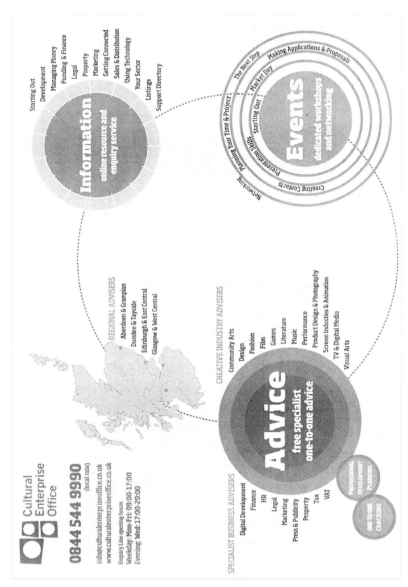

FIGURE 3.1 *Advice, Information and Events*[19]

provided client-centred administration for the full range of core activities, managing the bookings and record-keeping for workshop events as well as for the one-to-one sessions delivered by in-house advisers and freelance specialist advisers. The Business Support team also included the three in-house advisers, based in Glasgow, Edinburgh and Dundee. The much larger pool of freelance specialist advisers, who cover specific creative and business topics, are also affiliated to the Business Support team, with a dedicated part-time member of staff to manage their interactions with clients.

Figure 3.1 details how the range of core services was presented in CEO's internal and external documentation at the beginning of our engagement with the organisation in 2012. Apart from the fact that the Aberdeen office had closed before our research began, and the pool of specialist advisers had expanded, it more or less represents the shape of the core service that we encountered as we began our fieldwork.

Taking the flow of information as our starting point, the arrangement of the circular zones, with the client trajectory represented by the dotted line, reproduces graphically the routine gate-keeping practices observed when we shadowed the frontline Business Support staff. Clients' point of first contact or reconnection mostly occurs through the information service, by way of exploring the website, a phone call or an email enquiry, or some combination of these. In addition to dealing with the practicalities of the enquiry, the person taking phone calls and handling the incoming email enquiries – usually the Enquiries Officer – has a frontline diagnostic role: determining the need and creating or adding to the client's database record, as well as directing the client through the service.

As CEO pulled back from the Four Cities phase in 2010–2011, the role of the Enquiry and Information service began to be more centrally positioned as the primary way through which CEO could serve clients across the whole of Scotland. However, over the years, the range and volume of webpages, downloadable resources, FAQs, case histories, and relevant external links had grown hugely. This was not merely a case of the build-up over time of CEO-produced material; the support landscape had become more complex, and thus the task of organising, updating and maintaining online resources became increasingly time consuming and cumbersome for staff. Moreover, both in the real world and online, this complexity made navigating the support landscape confusing for clients. Therefore, much of the interactive work of the Enquiries role has been about bridging the gaps: matching clients to the information they need, the relevance of which they would struggle to identify for themselves. Inside CEO, the importance of the navigability of the online resources and the need for the website to represent its values and ethos effectively has been increasingly recognised. Chapter 5 addresses recent attempts to devise a new digital strategy.[20]

Support

Although there is no strict limit to the amount of support delivered to any one client, a typical trajectory through the core service portfolio is guided by a mixture of established procedures (based on judgements concerning potential and progress) and a dose of financial pragmatism. A new client will not be channelled directly to an advice session with one of the comparatively expensive freelance business or creative industry specialist advisers, nor to one of the more in-depth types of support offered by CEO's in-house advisers (Professional Development Planning or Coaching). Rather, following a phone conversation with the Enquiries Officer, a new client will usually be directed to existing online information resources or be booked onto a one-to-many workshop such as Starting Out. Alternatively, if there is no appropriate workshop coming up, or if the Enquiry Officer's evaluation deems it appropriate, the client may be booked in for a standard one-hour, one-to-one session in Glasgow, Edinburgh or Dundee, with a member of the in-house staff advising team.

In 2012–2013, CEO delivered 642 in-house 'general' advisory sessions and 352 specialist sessions.[21] Access to the specialist advisers is tightly controlled because, although free to the client, it is more costly to the organisation, and so is generally only recommended following one or more prior meetings with an in-house adviser. Furthermore, if the specialisms of in-house advisers align closely with a client's business, they may be used as a lower-cost source of specialist advice. In-house advisers, and the Business Support team more widely, also act as gate-keepers, controlling the flow of clients between the core service and programmes. While some applications to programmes were the result of clients responding directly to external publicity, existing users of the core services may often be channelled towards a specific programme by the Business Support team.

A key difference between in-house advisers and specialist advisers concerns the nature of the advice sessions. While each in-house adviser has a distinctive style of interaction, all are strongly aligned with the core values of CEO, sharing a conception of the purpose and limits of an advice session and a set of established practices for managing it effectively.[22] Specialist advisers, in contrast, are not fully inducted into the organisation upon recruitment, resulting in considerable variation in the styles of engagement adopted by individuals. Some expressed a desire to cultivate a closer relationship with CEO's Business Support team in order to develop a clearer sense of the core organisational mission, vision and values that they felt they should be embodying. From CEO management's perspective, however, the more detached position of the specialists is helpful. Part of specialists' value derives from their offering an outside, independent perspective, and CEO is reluctant to curtail their freedom to offer advice in the way they consider most relevant for their sector. Client expectations and individual adviser preferences (for instance, the etiquette of sharing or not sharing contacts), shape the nature of specialist advice interactions.

The other core service element is the portfolio of events: one of the most visible elements of CEO's practice.[23] Training workshops are designed to support creative practitioners at all stages of their careers, from Starting Out, which introduces creative practitioners to the how-to-do-its of setting up a business, to The Next Step, designed for creative practitioners who have been in business for more than two years. CEO also runs regular workshops tailored to support the development of specific skills, such as marketing, presentation and time management, and collaborates with external partners to deliver one off events, often with a focus on networking. These activities fall under the remit of the much smaller Events team. However, there are strong connections between the Events and Business Support teams.

Workshops have been an element of CEO's offer from the start. Most events that we observed had been formulated by Fiona Pilgrim, one of CEO's founding staff, with help from colleagues, in the mid-to-late 2000s. However, although they have been updated in part since that time, much of the material has remained unchanged since the events were first created. A key advantage of one-to-many events is that they enable a degree of efficiency; once designed, a workshop can be delivered many times. However, in a rapidly changing sector there is constant pressure to ensure relevance and utility. During our period of observation, many of CEO's events were, arguably, reaching the end of their useful lives. Creating new events – or even updating old ones – is an extremely time-consuming process. The demands on CEO staff members' time means that event slides cannot be routinely revised, hence the information on them may be out of date and frequently facilitators need to draw on their current knowledge of the sector in order to be up to date during the live delivery of the events.

Projects and partnership working

As noted, through its various phases CEO has also established a track record of working in partnership to deliver events and develop one off projects. Often these are focused on particular issues and designed to respond to a need expressed by clients. For example, in 2013 CEO worked in a partnership to deliver an event on finding and managing workspaces. CEO's client-facing staff had reported that this issue was assuming greater importance across the client base, and teamed up with WASPS in order to deliver an event. Alongside issue-focused events, CEO may also work in partnership to address art-form or sector-specific concerns. So, for instance, in March 2013 CEO delivered an event concerned with product design and development in partnership with the Lighthouse, Scotland's national centre for design and architecture. Each partnership event is handled differently, although CEO is usually the leading brand. Generally these events involve a registration fee, in contrast to CEO's own events, which are usually free. Working in partnership also introduces particular challenges, stemming from the fact that CEO and some of its partnership organisations have very different value systems, styles of communication, and modes of promotion. Consequently, some partnership events entail an ill fit between partners.

Alongside partnership working, CEO is often commissioned by other organisations to deliver events. It is regularly called upon to offer business training to final-year students at Scottish universities and for a fee will tailor and deliver Starting Out to small groups. Delivering such events to universities contributes to CEO's revenue stream. The staff are aware that training in business skills is still not integrated into creative degree programmes, usually coming late in the day, when students are preparing portfolios and entries for degree shows.

Developments in programmes

As we began our study, CEO was running the well-established Starter for 6 programme and had recently launched a second, more specialised, programme called Fashion Foundry. An incubator for fashion

DOI: 10.1057/9781137478887.0006

and textile designers, this aimed to capitalise on a recent resurgence in Scottish fashion by aiding business development in the high end and luxury sub-sector. Fashion Foundry was the first project to exploit CEO's new space. It was located in the same studio complex as CEO's office and led by CEO, in partnership with the organisation running the building, WASPS. Funded by Creative Scotland and Scottish Enterprise, it was among the first recipients of monies from Creative Scotland's Talent Incubator Programme, launched in 2011.

As has been demonstrated, ideas and practices can move into an agency such as CEO directly, through individuals such as consultants, as well as by establishing working partnerships with other bodies, as with NESTA. However, this process of influence can also happen at one remove, where new fashions in support practice arrive pre-approved, via funding schemes that promote particular models of operation. CEO has always been forced – by dint of its precarious funding position – to adhere closely to trends in creative business support, reshaping its objectives to fit with the latest funding pots to become available, both in order to maximise funding streams and to prove its currency and relevance within the creative sector. Nowhere has this been more evident than in the case of Fashion Foundry.

The incubator model is a relatively recent type of intervention in the field of business development. Pioneered by the Greater London Enterprise Board in the 1980s, it originally emerged as a primarily state-led venture, although as John Montgomery notes, there are increasing numbers of private sector managed workspaces across the UK.[24] The model is widely used as means to support start-ups and foster innovation by reducing the overheads for various kinds of small business. The incubator model is not, however, widely used in the creative sector and there is some debate over whether or not it is even a helpful intervention in the creative economy.[25] Montgomery notes that relatively few creative sector incubators are able to achieve sustainability, and most require a mix of public and private investment.[26]

Montgomery has identified two general models of creative sector incubator: those that generate revenue by charging rental space, and those that take a percentage of the income produced by the businesses using the space. As a pilot project, Fashion Foundry did not adhere closely to either of these. In its inaugural year, participants were charged a nominal bench fee, which entitled them to pairing with an industry mentor, business development advice from the project manager, and in six out of ten cases, space in a small studio one floor upstairs from CEO in South Block.

Fashion Foundry ran its inaugural cycle between September 2012 and March 2014, with ten businesses supported. The programme consisted of two elements: the incubator itself, which was accessed through a competitive application process, and a series of events open to both participants and to the wider designer fashion and textiles industry at all stages of their lifecycle – from pre-start-up businesses to established ventures.

By mid-2014, although committed to running another cycle of Fashion Foundry, CEO was taking an increasingly critical position on the incubator model. Our own research captured many of the practical frustrations of the programme for staff and clients, and a consultancy report commissioned by CEO from Sarah Thelwall and Yvonne Fuchs noted significant problems in the way that Fashion Foundry was initially conceived.[27] By supporting both fashion and textile businesses, there was confusion as to whether the incubator was there to help fashion businesses to make a name for themselves by innovating in design, or whether it was there to seed innovation in manufacturing. The consultants concluded that it was inefficient to support businesses concerned with both of these modes of innovation within the same project, and that it led to frustration on the part of the participants and staff involved.

Our period of observation also covered the development and launch of a new programme – ultimately named Flourish – designed to address the view that CEO was interested only in start-ups. This will be covered in Chapter 5.

Conclusion

The early history of CEO can be understood as a series of short-term projects – structured into discrete operational phases by a sequence of core funding packages. Each of these lasted a few years, had a set of objectives to be achieved, and left a legacy of values and practices in the organisation. As CEO diversified its offer and funding mix over the years, it gradually shifted from simply being a project to establishing itself as an organisation that manages a range of projects, simultaneously seeking to deliver its services according to multiple criteria, with overlapping deadlines and various external partners. The move, from being housed

DOI: 10.1057/9781137478887.0006

in an arts centre in 2002 to a creative sector studio complex in 2012, can also be understood as embodying a wider policy turn, from the cultural to the creative economy.

After 13 years in existence, CEO had shifted in geographic reach and ambition and in the scope and potential career stage of clients supported. It had gone from being a Glasgow-centred organisation to one seeking to serve the whole of Scotland. But the closure of the Aberdeen office in 2011 further concentrated the service within the Scottish central belt.[28] Nonetheless, the national ambition remained, and Chapter 5 will address the ways in which we observed this being reimagined through digital provision and partnership working.

The rapidly changing support landscape has also worked, in recent years, to erode some of the distinctiveness of CEO's delivery style. The methods by which CEO has encouraged clients to think about the development of their businesses are now widely diffused throughout the creative sector. Consequently, longer-serving staff observed that their clients were now far more familiar with the techniques and language of business than when CEO began. Other research has shown that creative practitioners' business skills have improved rapidly in recent years.[29] Therefore, as CEO has sought to refresh its events and other elements of its service, it has needed to keep pace with changing skillsets across the sector.

Another key feature of the most recent phase is that CEO began to think about how it might develop an independent policy voice by working to provide evidence of its knowledge of the sector and seeking to shift government thinking about the needs of creative micro-businesses. This was most visibly attempted through the work of Bob Last, who at the time was the Chair of CEO's Board. He undertook research into the value systems of successful micro-businesses and the financial challenges faced within the sector. Based in part on semi-structured interviews, this project has intersected with our own work, with Philip Schlesinger a member of its steering group, and is explored in greater detail in Chapter 5.

From this historical sketch, it is apparent that CEO's ability to bend and adapt, thus far, with the political and policy winds has enabled it to survive. By pursuing this shifting trajectory, the organisation has acquired a deep understanding of the challenges faced by the businesses it supports. Across CEO, and particularly for those front-line staff advising clients, constant organisational reinvention and the just-in-time nature of solutions to funding shortfalls have also contributed to an important,

DOI: 10.1057/9781137478887.0006

unstated shadow narrative, one in which the real precariousness of the organisation creates a fellow-feeling with the client base.

Much in the spirit in which it advises those businesses, CEO has made its own opportunities. However, the economic and policy landscape is still constantly changing and the succession of short-term, funding-driven goals and the growing importance of project-based working have also created internal challenges and tensions. Chapter 4 will examine how these are expressed in terms of organisational values and service delivery and then Chapter 5 will consider some specific ways in which CEO sought to reorientate itself for the future during 2013–2014.

Notes

1   O'Connor and Gu, 'Developing a creative cluster', 124.

2   Cultural Enterprise Office operated under the name Cultural Enterprise Unit until 2003, but for the sake of clarity it will be referred to as CEO throughout this book.

3   Cultural Enterprise and David Clarke Associates, *Feasibility study: to investigate the need for a specialist business support service for the cultural & creative industries in Glasgow* (Cardiff: Cultural Enterprise and David Clarke Associates, 1999).

4   John Myerscough, *Glasgow cultural statistics framework: digest of cultural statistics, a report commissioned by Glasgow City Council [3rd edition]* (Glasgow: Glasgow City Council, 1998). This quantitative evaluation framework for the cultural sector was commissioned initially in 1988 by Glasgow City Council from John Myerscough, and a digest has been produced every few years since.

5   CEO was not the only agency explicitly modelled on Cultural Enterprise Cardiff in 1999. The *Feasibility study* highlighted the Manchester-based initiative Creative Industries Development Service (CIDS, operational 2000–2008) as 'in development', following a similar piece of consultancy (see O'Connor and Gu, *Developing a creative cluster*).

6   The venue was Chapter, a Cardiff arts body that owned a large creative industries-focused studio space. They collaborated with pair of mainstream business support agencies: South Glamorgan Training and Enterprise Council and Business in the Community, with South Glamorgan TEC providing the initial money.

7   'Cultural Enterprise, paper presented to the Post-16 Education and Training Committee at Blackwood Miners Institute, High Street, Blackwood on 18 May 2000', The Welsh Assembly, accessed 9 March 2015, http://www.assembly. wales/en/.

DOI: 10.1057/9781137478887.0006

8   Scottish Enterprise Glasgow to Executive Team of Scottish Enterprise Glasgow, 20 June 2001, *Cultural Enterprise Unit [Internal recommendation document]*, Cultural Enterprise Office archive, Glasgow.

9   SQW, *Evaluation of the Cultural Enterprise Office: a project review and evaluation report to the Cultural Enterprise Office* (Edinburgh: SQW, 2006).

10   David Clarke Associates, *An interim evaluation of Cultural Enterprise Office Glasgow* (Cardiff: DCA, 2004).

11   David Clarke Associates, *An interim evaluation*.

12   A Cultural Enterprise Office draft business plan for 2005–2007 outlined the plan to scope more rural local authorities for interest in 'buying-in' to CEO's hub services, prefiguring the 'Cascade' plans outlined in Chapter 5.

13   'European Structural Funds', The Scottish Government, accessed 9 March 2015, http://www.scotland.gov.uk/Topics/Business-Industry/support/17404.

14   SWQ, *Evaluation*, 9–10.

15   In 2008–2009, 42 per cent of clients served were located in Glasgow and the West Central area and 36 per cent were located in Edinburgh and East Central. In the north east mainland, Tayside (which had an office in Dundee) and Grampian (with its office in Aberdeen) each accounted for only 6 per cent of clients respectively – the same as the sparsely populated and sprawling Highlands and Islands region covering the north west, which did not have a CEO office. South of the central belt, the rural Dumfries and Galloway accounted for the remaining 4 per cent. Cultural Enterprise Office, *Operating plan for 2010/2011* (Glasgow: Cultural Enterprise Office, 2010), 9.

16   A number of new internal projects also were developed in response to CEO staff's grounded perceptions of client needs. However, these met with mixed success. Common Turf was an online peer-networking platform (with a number of linked live networking events) that failed to flourish. Mentor Xchange sought to enable chains of peer mentoring, but floundered due to the fact it attracted a surfeit of potential mentees and was faced by a shortage of mentors. While PDP has remained part of the offer, the difficult experience of running two short-lived networking projects resulted in CEO being slow to engage in other forms of online networking and peer learning.

17   Workshop and Artists' Studio Provision Scotland Ltd.

18   In this respect CEO's new home echoed the set ups of the defunct Cardiff-based operation on which it was modelled and the Manchester-based CIDS agency (also closed) that had launched at roughly the same time as CEO. Cultural Enterprise and David Clarke Associates, *Feasibility study.*

19   Cultural Enterprise Office, *Operating plan*, 3. Until October 2014, in-house advisers were referred to both internally and externally as 'regional advisers'. 'Regional' was a legacy term, dating from the Four Cities phase, and was changed following our suggestion that it was no longer current and did not

DOI: 10.1057/9781137478887.0006

reflect the ways in which we had observed the expertise of these on-staff advisers being deployed.

20 A 2010 internal report on Information Services noted that for every unique user who contacted CEO in person another seven made use of the website material. In 2012–2013, CEO recorded 66,810 webpage visits from 34,344 unique visitors. CEO also tracks the reach of its video case studies and web article content through secondary sites. Social Value Lab, *Cultural Enterprise Office: performance and impact 2013/14 [December 2014 draft]* (Social Value Lab: Glasgow, 2014), 14.

21 Social Value Lab, *Cultural Enterprise Office: performance and impact,* 12.

22 The nature of this advisory work will be explored more fully in Chapter 4.

23 There were 660 separate workshop sessions run in 2012–2013. Starting Out was attended by 264 clients in 2012–2013. The Next Step was attended by just 22 in the same period. Social Value Lab, *Cultural Enterprise Office: performance and impact,* 13.

24 John Montgomery, 'Creative industry business incubators and managed workspaces: a review of best practice', *Planning Practice & Research* 22 (2007): 601–617.

25 Montgomery, 'Creative industry business incubators'; Joanna Belcher, Saskia Coulson and Louise Valentine, 'Making it happen: the role of design research in an emerging design museum', in *ESRC research capacity building clusters: summit conference 2013 (25–26 July, University of Aston) Proceedings,* eds. Ben Clegg, Judy Scully and John Bryson (Swindon: ESRC, 2013): 25–33.

26 Montgomery, 'Creative industry business incubators'.

27 Sarah Thelwall and Yvonne Fuchs, *Fashion Foundry & the wider set of creative industries talent incubators – a sustainability challenge. Report prepared for Creative Scotland and Cultural Enterprise Office* (Kingston: Sarah Thelwall, 2013).

28 Social Value Lab, *Performance and impact,* 5.

29 Scottish Government, *Creative industries, creative workers and the creative economy: a review of selected recent literature* (Edinburgh: Scottish Government, 2009).

4
Organisational Values and Practices of Support

Abstract: *This chapter takes a closer look at the business support practices of CEO, examining how the central ethos of the organisation is expressed through day-to-day client interactions and the language in which business advice is delivered and discussed. It identifies three core values underpinning the delivery of advice and support to clients – being bespoke, being non-judgemental and taking a coaching-centred approach to supporting clients – and considers the ways in which staff use the idea of 'client journeys' to conceptualise trajectories through CEO's service and the business world. Finally, it addresses the impact of the introduction of structured programmes on organisational values, arguing that these have introduced new terms and different styles of interaction to the organisation, reshaping the idea of 'being bespoke'.*

Keywords: business language; coaching; medical metaphors; organisational values

Schlesinger, Philip, Melanie Selfe and Ealasaid Munro. *Curators of Cultural Enterprise: A Critical Analysis of a Creative Business Intermediary.* Basingstoke: Palgrave Macmillan, 2015. DOI: 10.1057/9781137478887.0007.

As Chapter 3 has outlined, the shape and remit of CEO are the product of the organisation's gradual development within evolving local and national contexts of creative economy policy and an institutional landscape of cultural and business support structures. Different aspects of CEO's service were forged at different times in response to external agendas and internal imperatives. Over time, this has created a portfolio of support practices. CEO's own distinction between its core activities and programmes is central to understanding this. In particular, as the range of CEO's work has expanded, tension has developed between the way that relationships with clients are conceived and managed within the explicitly non-judgemental, demand-led approach to support embodied by the original core services as opposed to the more supply-led frameworks of the growing number of targeted programmes. Each of these has its own objectives, reflecting new priorities, distinctive values and shifting policy trends.

However, core activities and programmes are not entirely separate. Individual clients routinely move between the different elements of the service and given the way CEO delivers its core activities and programmes, these share staff, expertise and administrative systems. The basic systems and practices of CEO's core largely underpin the development and delivery of new programmes. Moreover, the traffic is not just one-way. Individual tools developed within programmes can find their way into the core, and programmes have also begun to exert a deeper influence on the way CEO sees its relationship to clients. During our period of observation, the Business Support team responsible for delivering the core activities was in the process of rethinking the 'client journey' in ways that seemed to lean increasingly towards the formats used by programmes.

This chapter seeks to tease out differences and areas of overlap between core activities and programmes, paying attention both to the intrinsic values of the older and newer elements of CEO's service before reflecting on the exchange of ideas between them. We shall explore how these differences of approach are expressed in everyday practice, specifically in relation to the working language used.

Many of the issues explored here are highly congruent with the brief observations made by O'Connor and Gu concerning CIDS in Manchester which, as noted in Chapter 3, was set up at a similar time and also based on the Cultural Enterprise Cardiff model. In particular, O'Connor and Gu highlight CIDS' role as a bespoke business support provider for the

DOI: 10.1057/9781137478887.0007

creative sectors, which both expressly set out to speak its clients' language and predominantly employed staff who were themselves drawn from world of creative labour rather than conventional business support. Like CEO, CIDS positioned itself as culturally 'bilingual', able to 'translate' both ways between creative and economic registers. However, reflecting on the Manchester organisation's demise, O'Connor and Gu note the tensions created by its being closely aligned with the sector while also needing to serve policy agendas responsive to 'box-ticking' economic metrics. O'Connor and Gu remark that 'speaking the dual languages of creative sector and public policy caused much disorientation within CIDS staff' and have concluded that '[p]ersonal commitment and sharing a "language" with the creative industries in the end could hardly make up for the lack of resources.'[1]

We observed similar tensions playing themselves out at CEO. On the one hand there was a deeply felt and strongly principled sense of being 'of and for' the sector and, on the other, an acute pressure to provide evidence of the organisation's value on the terms required by funders, which in turn were shaped by dominant policy discourses. In Chapter 5, we shall explore how, over the course of our fieldwork, CEO developed strategic plans to become more 'business-like' in its operations. However, our close observation of the organisation also permitted us to consider how these tensions played out in practice. We shall suggest that a third type of language also needs to be considered – that of support – which has been shaped both by the use of ad hoc metaphors as well as by the more deliberate adoption of professional rhetoric. This is how central tensions are expressed and negotiated, and the way that client interactions are managed on a daily basis.

Being bespoke: core services and values

While, confusingly, the term 'core' is sometimes used to refer to everything covered by CEO's general budget, such as marketing and administration, during our fieldwork in the organisation we quickly grasped that it is primarily applied to the central portfolio of services that has been part of CEO's offer from the outset and around which everything else has been built. More gradually, however, we also came to understand it as a set of underlying organisational *values* closely associated with these services. In Chapter 3, we outlined how the delivery of core

DOI: 10.1057/9781137478887.0007

services (information, one-to-one advice sessions and workshop events) is managed and fits into the structure of the organisation. Here, taking a different perspective, we shall examine how core services combine organisational practice and a specific ethos. This is expressed and reinforced through CEO's routine interaction with clients. The three facets of the core service are: being bespoke, being non-judgemental, and taking a coaching-centred approach to supporting clients.

In practice, these are all closely inter-related. As noted in Chapter 3, a number of the principles of interaction with clients date back to ideas put forward in the 1999 feasibility study that preceded the establishment of CEO. Perhaps the most important and pervasive of these inherited values is the idea of being non-judgemental, outlined below in relation to the original working practices of Cultural Enterprise Cardiff:

> Generally, we do not seek to judge the quality of our clients' work, or differentiate our level of service provision on the basis of artistic merit. We do, however, make judgements about the seriousness of our clients' commitment to making their businesses work and limit support in cases where the client is seeking to transfer responsibility to ourselves for moving things forward. Very occasionally this is made explicit to the client where, in our view, understanding why our assessment is that their business will not succeed will help them to build more successful relationships in the future.[2]

The distinction made between judging the artistic merit of the work and judging how committed and realistic the client is about developing and pursuing a business plan, has been replicated within CEO, but in practice it is a difficult line to maintain. The way in which an individual client is guided through the service and the level and type of support received will necessarily be informed by the way the CEO's staff understand the client's work and imagine its relationship to a potential market. However, although advisers and other front-line staff have deep knowledge of some fields and markets, other areas are less familiar. CEO now supports practitioners working across a much-expanded spectrum of the creative sectors. These include historically subsidised cultural sub-sectors, such as fine art, where artistic 'quality' and building a reputation among elite gatekeepers determine where one can sell one's work. But CEO also now covers more commercially-orientated creative industries, such as games, apps or product design, where key challenges concern funding and managing the various stages of product development.

Thus, while there is usually a balance to be struck between creative ambition and commercial viability, this varies greatly from client to

DOI: 10.1057/9781137478887.0007

client. Although it is not necessary for CEO staff to directly judge quality in the way that an arts council might, that kind of judgement still needs to be imagined at one remove: in effect, to ask how the market will ultimately value the work.

It is difficult for staff not to bring personal views and organisation-wide assumptions to bear in making such calls. CEO's personnel are acutely aware of this. In devising support scenarios they exhibit a wealth of expertise, built both from first-hand knowledge of their respective fields and many years of advising experience, but they are reluctant to position themselves as experts, acknowledging both the specificity of each field and the limitations of their own insight. In our fieldwork, we noted a self-conscious anxiety inside CEO about being sure to maintain a non-judgemental stance. This was sometimes expressed in terms of a concern not to jump to conclusions about clients, or not to misread their ambitions and potential. In support practice, this means that the principal matter that is being critically estimated (and actively supported) by CEO is clients' ability to present themselves, to undertake self-evaluation, and to hone the ability to communicate an understanding of their own work and potential market more clearly. Two further core principles evidently help CEO's staff to manage this issue: the idea of being bespoke foregrounds tailoring the service to the client's need; the principle of coaching seeks to ensure that the decision-making process – and the responsibility for moving things forward – lies firmly and clearly with the client, positioning the CEO staff member as a facilitator who bring things out rather than acting as an expert or a judge.

The client journey

From its inception, CEO has emphasised a model of delivery that is highly client-centred and bespoke. Consequently, the core services are designed to provide support to clients as and when required. These services are framed as a flexible interlocking resource, rather than as a linear course to be run: they constitute a series of elements that can be navigated differently, according to each individual's business development need. But the way in which clients navigate the service is necessarily shaped and directed by a series of formal and informal structures. Therefore, it is important to understand not only what is delivered by each aspect of the core offer but also how the various possible client journeys through the service elements are envisaged and managed by CEO staff.

DOI: 10.1057/9781137478887.0007

As noted in Chapter 3, the point of first contact for most clients is via the website and email or through the enquiry line. From this point, the Business Support team work to guide the client to the most appropriate service. Particularly in relation to phone enquiries, the process of evaluating client need involves working nimbly across the somewhat cumbersome Client Record Management (CRM) system, in combination with other online resources. The Enquiries Officer will locate the client's record in the database – which contains accounts of previous interactions with CEO – while simultaneously bringing up the caller's own website in order to gain a picture of the business and its public face. These digital representations of the client, visible across multiple open browser tabs, are combined with the phone conversation under way, and feed into the Enquiry Officer's rapid assessment of the caller's current business status and support needs. Consequently, this role wields a lot of influence in terms of shaping and curating the client's relationship to the organisation.

Each interaction by phone, email or in person contributes to the cumulative record held for each client, and accounts of enquiries are joined by copies of client communications as well as post-session adviser reports, to create the picture of the client's relationship with the organisation. However, this is necessarily partial. With an eye to data protection issues, the content and tone of staff accounts is deliberately cautious – the guidelines state that these should remain strictly factual and positive – and while there is greater variety in both interaction and reporting styles across the specialist advisers than the in-house advisers, an administrative, gate-keeping layer ensures that the written reports supplied to clients and added to the record by freelance advisers also conform to the same standards. Inevitably, these restrictions exclude from the official record much of what is disclosed by clients and understood by advisers about the challenges of creating and sustaining a living in a creative field. Thus, more informal mechanisms are also crucial to the way knowledge is circulated and built up within the organisation.

Although, ideally, CEO's services are bespoke – meaning that each client should be able to pick and choose from the services on offer, depending on individual need – in reality, staff recognise that there are well-worn pathways, or journeys through the service. These client journeys serve a variety of functions inside the organisation. First, because there are limited opportunities for front-line staff to share knowledge about issues affecting the sector, they often share the breadth of their

DOI: 10.1057/9781137478887.0007

knowledge by discussing the case of a single client and that person's journey. This functions as a way of feeding back adviser expertise into the larger pool of Business Support staff. Second, if particular clients have performed particularly well in the sector, their journeys can become a template for other up and coming individuals, who may be set on the same path, in the hope of replicating earlier success. Although CEO's staff recognise that there is no universal template for success, some client journeys do become models for support. Contrariwise, some client journeys become well known and oft-repeated cautionary tales. For instance, a client's business may have started brightly but stalled because of poor decision-making or a failure to find adequate support.

Client journeys also play a role in terms of CEO's desire to demonstrate the worth of intermediary organisations and their interventions in the creative economy, in line with our analysis in Chapter 2. In this respect, particularly successful clients provide advertising for CEO and its services. A stellar client who credits CEO – even in part – with playing a role in their success, and who is able to cogently tell the story of their development, is an eye-catching way to showcase the efficacy of creative business support. Client journeys may therefore also function as tools for communicating the worth of intervention in the creative economy to a variety of audiences – potential and existing clients, funders, government, and policy-makers.

Advising and the language of support

Early in our fieldwork, we noted the frequency with which client-facing CEO staff employed medical language in order to describe and explain their relationship with clients. While this was often informal, it was also in places consolidated into the formal terminology. For instance, the follow-on support for Starter for 6 is titled 'aftercare' and, when deciding what is needed by a client who is making an enquiry, the front-line business support team refers to the diagnostic process as 'triage'. This medical term is not uncommon in customer service contexts, but it is nonetheless telling.[3] The 'bleeding patient' has been recorded as a dominant metaphor in business crisis contexts, in relation to the frameworks favoured by 'change agents' seeking to turn struggling businesses around,[4] and more broadly, in business media reporting practices.[5] In terms of the CEO staff role, triage entails that they use their considerable expertise to make a quick, efficient evaluation. But there is also the implication that for those requiring more substantial attention, the Enquiry staff are there

DOI: 10.1057/9781137478887.0007

primarily to stabilise things and the more substantial work will be done by the advisers at a later point. The concept of triage also potentially attaches an idea of crisis or emergency to the client enquiry.

In addition to the front-line term triage, it was routine for staff to position themselves more informally as providing forms of therapeutic support for creative practitioners. The model of the therapist-patient relationship is a powerful cultural trope that speaks to individuals' desire for self-improvement and unconditional support, and so it is perhaps unsurprising that interactions between advisers and clients often came to resemble therapy.[6] In CEO, giving therapy was recognised as problematic territory – the point at which an advice session was in danger of straying into areas where the staff had neither the remit nor the resources to provide help. However, it was also understood as inevitable that, in some cases, the relationship would play out this way. Starting and sustaining a creative enterprise is notoriously precarious. CEO's staff reported that the straitened economic climate had made matters worse, with many clients finding themselves under increasing financial pressure, often struggling to survive. Staff also discreetly remarked upon a rise in mental health problems due to economic hardship.

In this context, clients often felt unable to make decisions pertaining to their businesses, as all of the options open to them appeared risky, and high stakes. Therefore, advisers were required to provide both practical and emotional support. In doing this work, much of the empathy engendered by the 'We are our clients' position taken by CEO staff was rooted in their identifying themselves as occupying the role of adviser-practitioner. It was grounded in the assumption that the clients' creative work was more than just a job or a business venture; it was also deeply woven into their sense of self and more often than not, the fabric of their home lives. In many cases, this was clearly true. The in-house advice sessions that we observed occasionally became emotional and discussions with specialist advisers confirmed that this was also the case in their own advisory work. Tears shed by clients were not an unusual feature of one-to-one advice sessions. In such situations, advisers displayed considerable emotional intelligence in order first, to investigate what was troubling the client, and second, to help the client instigate a plan of action. All of the advisers that we spoke to and observed had the ability to support upset or, at times, angry clients, and clearly engaged in forms of emotional labour[7] – that is, they undertook the difficult task of being emotionally supportive, while also working to help the client

DOI: 10.1057/9781137478887.0007

to make business decisions, often in extremely stressful circumstances. Some advisers appeared more comfortable with this style of engagement than others. Particularly for some freelance specialist advisers, the need for a broader skillset and a deeper support infrastructure for managing the challenges of dealing with emotional clients engendered the wish for more training in CEO's practices and approaches.

The concepts of therapy and triage also cut to the heart of the question of whether or not CEO's role is to make qualitative judgements. Therapy is oriented towards ensuring a return to health (assuming therefore, that there is a malaise) and, for its part the medical metaphor of triage entails making a judgement. Triage is not just about prioritising those most in need; it is also about deciding who cannot be helped. The recognition that sometimes clients simply would not benefit from CEO's services recurred in many of our conversations with in-house advisers and other Business Support staff. Those who did not take advice and who failed to progress between sessions came to be viewed as problem clients and their journeys became cautionary tales.

Continuing to support such 'needy' clients was seen as both a poor investment of CEO's time and resources and ultimately, not good for those concerned. 'Problem' clients were often discussed in terms of their lack of real world awareness, a framing which encompassed a failure on their part to evaluate self-critically both the artistic quality and business potential of their own work. This critique was often most readily applied to the self-taught client who lacked the markers of a formal arts practice education and the visible field-specific social competence demonstrated by an extended creative network that might help to provide them with a reality check on their creative and business practice. However, there was also recognition that it was important to be open to supporting self-taught practitioners. While these might be regarded as isolated and unschooled, they might also have exceptional talent and a good commercial idea.

As we have noted, in some ways CEO can be understood as a translation service, however, in other respects the practitioner status of the majority of staff, and their first-hand knowledge of the difficulty of making creative practice pay, may also work to reinforce the divide between commerce and art. Although CEO staff understood the current economic environment as inflicting wounds on the body of the business, they believed that the client's creative self or 'soul' still needed to be nurtured. This tension between the requirement to be sympathetic

DOI: 10.1057/9781137478887.0007

and supportive and the need to give potentially brutal, business-savvy counsel was clearly observed during clients' in-house advice sessions and other interactions with advisers.

Reflecting on this difficulty at a staff meeting, one in-house adviser described the difficulties inherent in advising those who had 'done everything right' but who were still failing. She solicited advice from the other in-house advisers present, asking whether it was ever appropriate to advise 'killing the business' (what one does) in order to 'save the artist' (what one inherently is). Of course, views regarding the need for therapy as opposed to the first aid of practical business advice are profoundly affected by given advisers' knowledge of the problems facing different sectors, and the complex interplay of other factors such as how age, experience, and education might affect the client's status and ability to progress.

Many clients balance a complex mix of activities, often undertaking more commercial work or an element of teaching to enable the continuation of financially unproductive but artistically rewarding practices. One thing that differentiates CEO from other business support agencies is its willingness to address the portfolio structure of its clients' creative lives. This means CEO understands that there may be value in continuing with work that is not directly profitable (such as a jeweller making a few high-priced gallery pieces), both for reasons of personal artistic development and satisfaction and for the reputational rewards which may ultimately help to increase what can be charged for their work. But this more integrated view of the creative practitioner and the creative business makes advising very complex. One of the key challenges of supporting clients' decision-making processes is that it is not just a question of knowing when to 'persevere or pivot' – namely, when to redouble effort and plough on or when to change tack – but also, due to the portfolio nature of activities, knowing around which element of the work to pivot or which to push forward.

Here, when critical decisions that will affect both the business viability and personal satisfaction of the client are at stake, the increasing importance of the coaching model in CEO becomes particularly significant. CEO's staff are acutely aware of the limitations of the support they can actually provide. There are no right answers, everything is a trade-off, and the hard decisions all need to be taken and 'owned' by the client. The aim, in the end, is to help clients define their own priorities and to devise a suitable strategy for them to take responsibility for their decisions.

DOI: 10.1057/9781137478887.0007

Recent organisation-wide training in coaching techniques appears to have offered CEO staff a way to professionalise and thereby contain the amount of emotional labour that they undertake, thus providing support that does not tip over into the problematic territory of therapy.

A coaching-centred approach

In recent years the principles of coaching have been deliberately embedded throughout the organisation. A long-standing member of the advisory staff, who had previously worked as a life coach, incorporated elements of coaching practice into her work early on. More recently, all of the in-house advisers were trained and accredited as coaches and used the principles of active listening and reflective questioning in their standard advising practice. CEO's Director, Deborah Keogh, had also been an advocate of this practice since she herself underwent professional coaching. Thus, through the influence of these key staff members, the coaching approach has come to underpin the wider staff-client interaction style across the whole of CEO. However, during the year in which we studied the organisation, what had initially been a background ethos and approach was drawn to the fore, to be applied as an explicit technique, through the decision to train all staff to accredited level by using the services of Relational Dynamics 1st (RD1st), a company providing training in leadership and coaching with a specific emphasis on the arts sector.

Key coaching principles include keeping a focus on facilitating self-directed learning rather than providing answers. The RD1st model makes a distinction between the goal-orientated nature of coaching and the open-ended, emotionally exploratory format of therapy. It also distinguishes coaching from the more advice-centred expert role taken in mentoring or teaching. In coaching, clients are encouraged to articulate their own objectives for the session. The coach then works non-judgementally with every client to identify obstacles and enables each of them to develop an independent solution in a way that avoids a sense of dependency.

The practice of coaching is located in a broader spectrum of psychological therapeutic techniques critiqued for promoting individualisation.[8] This intersects with a growing body of work that considers the restructuring of the non-profit and voluntary sectors on market principles and points to how different kinds of training practice and organisational culture contribute to this.[9] Reflecting on the professionalisation of other types of third sector organisation and their increasing co-option into state-defined social and civic roles, Nicholas Fyfe has observed that 'Glasgow perhaps more than any other UK city has increasingly come to be represented in academic discourses in terms of a transition from the urban managerialism of the "welfare city" to the urban entrepreneurialism of the "neo-liberal city".[10]

Molly George has explored the emergence of life coaching in the US in the last three decades, where this is conceived as an 'expert service worker' occupation (simultaneously 'frontline' and highly skilled).[11] She has suggested that life coaches have emerged in response to the precariousness of work in an increasingly insecure employment market. This creates both the demand for the service, as clients seek the skills and confidence to build their lives and careers in self-directed ways, while also – on the supply-side – giving an entrepreneurial incentive to those seeking to train as coaches. In their discussion of the relative lack of attention afforded to questions of labour in cultural policy in Canada and Europe, Catherine Murray and Mirjam Gollmitzer[12] similarly explore business support strategies that encourage self-management, noting that these are often about making people adapt to a precarious labour market, rather than encouraging advocacy or collective action regarding poor working conditions.

The form of coaching delivered by CEO is professionally focused. In both commercial businesses and public sector organisations, executive coaching has been used extensively to try to improve productivity and managerial flexibility in rapidly changing environments. The precarious creative sector has been slower to turn to coaching than more mainstream sectors. According to one well-placed expert in the field, New Labour's investment in arts leadership in the mid-2000s was a turning point.[13] Schemes such as Arts Council England's Cultural Leadership Programme and the Clore Leadership Programme had both engaged established business coaches. However, it rapidly became apparent that coaching would not be sustainable beyond the life of such well-funded leadership fellowships because arts organisations simply could not afford to remunerate coaches at the same rate as their corporate clients. Deb Barnard, the trainer who delivered CEO's whole-team training sessions developed RD1st in part, at least, to provide a service at a price more affordable by the public and third sectors. She also took the view that the arts should 'grow their own' coaching expertise and employ trainers with arts backgrounds. Like CEO, RD1st has set out to market first-hand sector-specific experience to its clients.

DOI: 10.1057/9781137478887.0007

The impact of coaching training was especially evident among the more junior frontline staff at CEO. Their newly acquired skills were explicitly and positively invoked in a number of client interactions. The dissemination of coaching skills across the organisation began to address the diffidence we observed when non-advising staff were plainly very cautious about not overstepping their role by offering advice and support, particularly if their clients were working in fields radically different from their own practical experience. That caution was apparent even if their accumulated knowledge and experience meant that they could have guided the client appropriately. Their new coaching skills, and conscious reflection upon these, seemed to provide a welcome critical distance, helping them to reposition both the problems raised and the solutions offered as legitimately belonging to the client and giving staff more confidence to address these.

Programming new priorities, keeping core values

The addition of programmes has reshaped CEO, making its service delivery more complex and introducing new values and operational procedures. Having already described Starter for 6 and Fashion Foundry in Chapter 3, we now consider the most recently-introduced of the three programmes current during our research, Flourish. This focused on achieving sustainability for established businesses, and was developed and launched during our period of observation in 2013. During Flourish's initial cycle, it was evident that there was a mismatch between the new priorities embodied by the programme, and the older, core values that had come to represent such a key element of CEO's brand. However, as we will show, Flourish differed in several key aspects from CEO's other, more established programmes.

Flourish

Whereas new programmes have been devised in relation to CEO's take on the sector's needs, they have also been created in relation to shifting trends in creative economy policy (as well as being attendant on changing fashions in intervention styles) outlined in Chapter 2. New programmes also often incorporate and deploy a distinct idiom, reflecting new sector priorities. In the case of Starter for 6, for example, this involved reorientation towards the idea of innovation, whereas with Flourish the keyword was sustainability.

Interviews conducted with clients and stakeholders suggested that CEO was seen as offering fairly basic business advice, with many interviewees intimating that CEO was 'just for start-ups'. In April 2013, not long after we entered the field, we discovered that the finishing touches were being put to Flourish, which ran for nine months, and was designed to support the founders of 12 established businesses. To be eligible, founders had to be able to draw an income from their businesses, and the business needed to have been trading for two or more years.

Flourish was based on NESTA's Creative Business Mentor Network, launched in 2009.[14] Many features were shared by the Creative Business Mentor Network and CEO's version of the programme – for example, in both programmes a key condition was that businesses were required to demonstrate their potential for internationalisation. However, several key changes needed to be made in order to ensure its 'fit' with the Scottish context. First, as with Starter for 6, the programme needed to be recalibrated to take in the breadth of the creative sector: the Creative Business Mentor Network supported businesses from five key creative industries only (advertising, film, TV, digital media and games), whereas Flourish – like CEO's services more generally – encompassed the breadth of the DCMS categories. Second, NESTA's mentor programme focused primarily on those creative sector businesses with the potential for high growth, namely with a turnover of £1m or more. However, imposing such a restriction on Flourish would have drawn CEO away from its stated focus on micro-businesses; instead, as noted above, Flourish required business founders only to be able to draw an income from their businesses, with no minimum turnover cited. Third, where NESTA's programme required businesses to have been trading for three years or more, Flourish required only two years' trading.

The Flourish programme consisted of three training events, either held in or near to prominent Scottish companies' headquarters or manufacturing facilities. The purpose of this proximity was to enable CEO to conduct site visits with Flourish businesses, as part of a wider push (noted earlier in our discussion of Fashion Foundry) to encourage business owners to take advantage of opportunities in Scotland, rather than looking elsewhere for inspiration.

Unusually for CEO – which in the past had either 'imported' whole programmes (Starter for 6), or developed them largely in-house (Fashion

DOI: 10.1057/9781137478887.0007

Foundry) – Flourish combined an external template (developed by NESTA) with training events designed and led by an external trainer, with a background in digital media training. This was the first time that CEO had commissioned an external partner to design and deliver a full programme of training events. As will be seen later, the language, tone and content of the Flourish training events was notably different from anything else observed during our research, and offered a stark contrast to the therapeutic language encountered elsewhere in CEO's service.

In addition to training events and site visits, Flourish businesses were also paired with a creative industry mentor whose role was to offer support and advice throughout the programme. The businesses also received specialist business advice as part of the programme, drawn from CEO's internal pool of advisers and managers.

We interviewed members of staff involved in Flourish's development, and conducted direct observation at Flourish events. What was striking about these was the relative lack of attention afforded to questions of creativity. Rather, the focus at all of the Flourish events we observed was on business growth. Participants were spoken to first as business owners and only second as creative practitioners. Participants recognised the utility of the programme. However, the lack of attention given to questions of creativity – in other words, the underlying assumption that a creative business functioned much like any other business – emerged as a bone of contention. One reason for this was the evident lack of fit between the values embodied by Flourish and those embedded within core services. Of course, most of the Flourish clients were very familiar with CEO's approach, and the ethos of its day-to-day activities.

As noted in Chapter 3, where we discussed Fashion Foundry, any pilot programme is bound to suffer operational teething problems. In the development phase of Flourish, CEO had struggled to recruit suitable mentors. NESTA's supplementary research material – commissioned for the Creative Sector Mentor Network – noted that while 66 per cent of creative sector businesses wished to be involved with a mentor, only 58 per cent of established businesses were willing to supply one.[15] The problem of recruiting quite enough mentors appeared to be a common one for the sector. The lack of standardisation of mentor-client relationships also emerged as a problem, with some mentors initially unwilling to sign contracts detailing due diligence. Some, though, invested considerably more time and effort in their mentees than others. Given that the mentoring relationship was a central tenet of the programme, the varying experiences of client participants gave the CEO staff managing the mentoring element of Flourish some cause for concern.

A further problem for some participants we spoke to concerned the volume of work required by the programme. Many of the businesses that participated in Flourish were sole traders, some of whom had more than one job. Participants were asked to sign a contract at the beginning of the programme committing them to attend every session, and also to complete between-session 'homework' assignments. Several stated that this was an unreasonable workload. One member of CEO's staff observed that this was symptomatic of how many creative practitioners viewed business skills, as 'something that you can learn later, or relegate to second place. In reality, your "business head" is every bit as important as your "creative head".'[16]

As noted above, Flourish also represented CEO's first foray into commissioning content and employing an external trainer, and this created undoubted issues of language compatibility and fit with CEO's established house style. These were common concerns across CEO's portfolio of programmes, although in Flourish they were arguably exacerbated due to the presence of an outsider and, of course, the newness of the programme. We therefore witnessed CEO's staff moving quickly to dissolve tensions on the ground, smoothing over the cracks between the values embedded in the programme and CEO's core values.

The impact of programmes

As our examination of Flourish demonstrates, individual programmes have their own logics, languages and styles of interaction. Different programmes came with different sets of expectations regarding the participants best suited to them, and consequently, different ideas of the ideal client trajectory. For instance, while Starter for 6, which was aimed primarily at pre-start-up businesses, assumed that participants required speedy growth, Flourish instead focused on internationalisation and made clear the importance of sustainability for established businesses. Clients that fitted such model trajectories could be used as case studies, demonstrating CEO's impact within the sector.

The creative sector is sometimes characterised as a collaborative economy, reliant on sharing and barter, and on building relationships within sectors, clusters and networks.[17] For the most part, CEO aligned itself with this broad viewpoint, and made it part of the everyday work of client support. However, at times CEO also departed from the script. For example, Starter for 6 sometimes seemed to be heavily influenced by pop-cultural representations of business, which jarred with what we observed of other elements of the CEO support portfolio. This was most striking in the Starter for 6 pitching process, which was presented as extremely high-stakes, and bore a marked resemblance to television programmes such as *Dragon's Den*. Unquestionably, the growing cultural awareness of languages of business and entrepreneurship has been mediated by such programmes and profoundly shaped by entertainment values. Both clients and invited experts completely recognised the 'pitch to panel' set-up which was modelled on the TV format and thus slipped into versions of a highly adversarial public script.[18]

Entry to CEO's programmes is competitive, involving a substantial investment of time and resources, and in the case of Starter for 6, the possibility of some investment. This has led to a potential conflict with one of the founding values established in the core services, that of abstaining from judgements about the quality of clients' creative work. Of course, in the course of offering core services critical evaluations are made of each client's suitability for CEO support and the types of help from which they might benefit. This starts as soon as the Enquiry Officer first picks up the phone or opens an email. The core team are able to support any client to some degree, regardless of whether the work is particularly original, innovative or commercial, or indeed, whether the business seems to be on track for growth. By approaching each client as a creative practitioner, CEO's staff could provide frank advice to those for whom the prospects did not seem auspicious. Ultimately the onus is on the client to make the final judgement about whether a particular business idea is viable or whether there is too high a cost involved for the creative autonomy desired. In contrast, where programmes are concerned, a specific budget is at stake. Consequently, CEO's staff cannot avoid making critical judgements about each client's suitability for what is on offer.

Although programmes are in most respects free-standing, they do influence the support given by core staff, not just at the level of disseminating new tools but also by supplying distinct models of practice.[19] As the core Business Support team worked to create clearer templates for client journeys at the start of 2014, there was a move towards providing more structured routes through the core resources, a shift clearly

DOI: 10.1057/9781137478887.0007

informed by the shape of programmes, and supported by the development of the new website. Although programmes had the potential to influence core practice they were not expected radically to alter it, or to impact negatively on CEO's brand, image, or position in the sector.

Each of the three programmes considered here and in Chapter 3 contained aspects of CEO's core offer. Starter for 6 was structured around a programme of events; Fashion Foundry incorporated coaching; and Flourish provided an example of commissioning an outside partner to develop licensed content for delivery. However, there were also fundamental ways in which the programmes challenged – as well as extended – CEO's customary ways of working.

Conclusion

There is a contrast between CEO's relationship to clients in its core activities and its programmes. Whereas both have aimed to deal with clients holistically and offer an understanding of the complexity of creative lives, there are differences in how support has been delivered. In the programmes, the focal unit of support is *the business*. By contrast, the core services remain shaped by the original aim: to make early-stage clients 'business-ready' by assisting them to develop a mixture of entrepreneurial strategies to support their creative work. Sometimes, this is achieved by helping clients (at any stage) to balance their lives through a portfolio of ventures. In this case, the focal unit of support is the *creative practitioner*. These differences are neither made explicit nor necessarily even clearly recognised by staff. Clients have the same kinds of entry on the database, and may move between core and programmes over the course of a relationship with the organisation, encountering the same staff in diverse contexts. Nonetheless, there is a significant, if implicit, difference between the way clients are positioned by the core and programme services. This reflects the distance travelled between CEO's point of origin and the creative economy framework which has since become dominant, within which the various programmes have been developed.

Moreover, the existence of distinctive programmes has begun to redefine the bespoke relationship between CEO and its clients. A programme, once funded, must be filled, run, and reported on. This means that clients must be found to fit a new programme's criteria. Those selected are regarded as able to succeed in the terms defined by the funder.

DOI: 10.1057/9781137478887.0007

Therefore, although programmes are tailored to meet a perceived sector need they also work to fit clients into broader policy agendas. CEO's commitment to being bespoke for the client has been complicated by the fact that there are always two interests to be satisfied: those of the individual creative practitioner and those of CEO's funders, whose policy-driven imperatives have shaped specific aspects of its service. However, these tensions are most acute and more visible in programmes, when it becomes legitimate to ask to what extent a given programme meets the needs of its users and to what degree it is tailored to instrumental goals coming from above.

Such tensions are evident from how the language used by programmes often contrasts with that used by core services. In both Starter for 6 and Flourish, the primary focus has been on business, with less of an emphasis on creativity. By contrast, what we observed of core activities was a predominant focus on the creative individual, with business advice framed in terms of enabling creativity, thereby allowing individuals to keep doing what they loved. As noted, one of the ways in which CEO has defined itself is as a translation service that helps creative practitioners to understand and speak the language of business. The reluctance – whether real or imagined – of creative practitioners to speak that way has often been identified as a problem for the creative sector. Whether or not creative practitioners should be expected to communicate fluently in business talk was regularly raised during the course of our research. The debate about expression, at times, is a proxy for that about cultural value.

Notes

1   O'Connor and Gu, 'Developing a creative cluster', 131.
2   David Clarke Associates, *An interim evaluation*, 55.
3   The *Oxford English Dictionary* defines 'triage' as follows: 'the assignment of degrees of urgency to wounds or illnesses in order to decide the order or suitability of treatment'.
4   Achilles Armenakis et al., 'Symbolism use by business turnaround change agents', *International Journal of Organizational Analysis* 4 (1996): 123
5   Michael O'Mara-Shimek, Manuel Gillén-Parra and Anna Ortega-Larrea, 'Stop the bleeding or weather the storm? Crisis solution marketing and the ideological use of metaphor in online financial reporting of the stock market crash of 2008 at the New York Stock Exchange', *Discourse and Communication* 9 (2014): 103.

DOI: 10.1057/9781137478887.0007

6   Eva Illouz, *Saving the modern soul: therapy, emotions, and the culture of self-help* (Berkeley CA: University of California Press, 2008).

7   Arlie Russell Hochschild, *The managed heart: the commercialization of human feeling* (Berkeley, CA: University of California Press, 1983).

8   Nikolas Rose, *Governing the soul: the shaping of the private self* (London: Free Association, 1989).

9   Sam, Binkley, 'Psychological life as enterprise: social practice and the government of neo-liberal interiority', *History of the Human Sciences* 24 (2011): 83; Heidi Marie Rimke, 'Governing citizens through self-help literature', *Cultural Studies* 14 (2000): 61; Katariina Mäkinen, 'The individualization of class: a case of working life coaching', *The Sociological Review* 62 (2014): 821.

10   Nicholas Fyfe, 'Making space for "neo-communitarianism"? The third sector, state and civil society in the UK', *Antipode* 37 (2005): 536.

11   Molly George, 'Seeking legitimacy: the professionalization of life coaching', *Sociological Enquiry* 83 (2013): 179.

12   Catherine Murray and Mirjam Gollmitzer, 'Escaping the precarity trap? A call for creative labour policy', *International Journal of Cultural Policy* 4 (2012): 419.

13   Interview, 23 March 2014.

14   'NESTA creative business mentor network: register your interest', NESTA, accessed 15 January 2015, http://www.nesta.org.uk/project/creative-business-mentor-network/full-details.

15   NESTA, *Mentoring in the creative sector: industry insights* (London: NESTA, 2014), 5–9.

16   Field note, 23 November 2013.

17   Mark Banks, 'Moral economy and cultural work', *Sociology* 40 (2000): 455.

18   Boyle and Kelly, *The television entrepreneurs.*

19   One instance occurred in Starter for 6. To ensure that the programme remained useful for clients, Starter for 6 staff needed to keep up to date with new trends in the teaching of entrepreneurship. The research team observed a staff meeting in June 2013 where one member of Starter for 6 staff reported on a seminar she attended on Lean Management (see 'What is Lean?', Lean enterprise institute, accessed 3 February 2015, http://www.lean.org/whatslean/). A summary of the principles of Lean Management was first fed into Starter for 6, and subsequently made available to core staff. This member of staff also developed a new tool for clients titled 'Talk To Your Market'. This tool was also trialled in Starter for 6, before subsequently being made available to core staff.

DOI: 10.1057/9781137478887.0007

5
Future-Proofing CEO?

Abstract: *This chapter addresses CEO's strategic development during 2013–2014, aided in part by targeted funding. In a bid to future-proof the organisation in an increasingly competitive business support landscape, CEO was restructured. It began to develop critical independent research, and sought to reimagine models of digital and physical service delivery. The bid for further Creative Scotland funding that would have enabled the more ambitious plans to be pursued was unsuccessful. This chapter explores the development of new goals when their realisation was still thought feasible, considers internal transformations observed in CEO as it attempted to prepare for this next phase, and reflects on the tension between serving and shaping the top-down policy agenda. The chapter contains a statement from the Director on her departure.*

Keywords: Creative Scotland; digital transformation; funding; organisational change; strategy

Schlesinger, Philip, Melanie Selfe and Ealasaid Munro. *Curators of Cultural Enterprise: A Critical Analysis of a Creative Business Intermediary.* Basingstoke: Palgrave Macmillan, 2015. DOI: 10.1057/9781137478887.0008.

After a decade of incremental change and continuous reshaping, largely dictated by the pressures of capturing and retaining external funding, by 2012 CEO was actively seeking a more stable and sustainable model of operation. It had effectively, if informally, made the transition from being a recurring project to becoming a continuous operation, but it had yet to acquire the kind of long-term, strategic planning and the infrastructure required to support this. Thus, there was an acute awareness of the need to rethink its organisational structure, reimagine models of service delivery and future-proof the organisation to remain relevant within an increasingly competitive business support landscape. But the most pressing issue – and the matter on which the ability to proceed with any emerging plans depended – was to secure adequate finance.

Throughout its existence, one of the biggest challenges facing CEO has been how to think, plan and operate like an organisation with a secure future, when it has never known if it has one. During 2013–2014, a key goal was to obtain a three-year award from Creative Scotland's Regular Funding scheme (spanning 2015–2018). This was coupled with the ambition to secure charity status, opening the door to tax breaks and reduced costs, and to diversify the organisation's business model and funding mix, reducing the overall reliance on public money as expressly desired by the Scottish Government. However, core Creative Scotland funding was still seen as central to success, underpinning the shorter grants and projects and crucially enabling more ambitious future focused development.

While the success of this major funding bid was never taken for granted, as CEO was already the recipient of this type of funding there was no obvious reason to consider a repeat award unlikely. Ultimately, however, the October 2014 funding announcement brought disappointment. Creative Scotland took the strategic decision to focus its three-year funding pot on organisations directly involved in cultural production activities, moving CEO and a range of other sector support organisations onto shorter term targeted funds.[1] For the period 2014–2015, CEO was defined as an 'Annual Client', in receipt of £487,000.[2] This sum enabled the agency to remain operational, but at this time of writing, CEO was still adjusting to this challenge to its plans for developing the service it offered. On 20 February 2015, the Director, Deborah Keogh, decided to move on.

Many of the more ambitious plans we observed CEO develop during our research could not come to fruition given the cut in hoped-for funding, which required severe retrenchment at the organisation.

DOI: 10.1057/9781137478887.0008

What follows, therefore, is our account of CEO's preparation for a quite different imagined future. Our aim is to explore the development of new goals when their realisation was still considered feasible and to consider the internal transformations we observed CEO undergo as it attempted to ready itself for this next phase.

First, however, it is worth considering the context of CEO's strategic planning more closely. By 2013, CEO was operating with its largest staff ever, which made instilling a collective sense of purpose and direction essential, but this was increasingly difficult in light of the organisation's continuing precariousness. Second, due to the accumulated range and volume of activities, the organisation was overstretched. Intensive labour was needed to patch over the inefficiencies caused by dated operational routines and IT systems. The staff were delivering more types of support, more frequently, but they no longer had the time to invest in developing new content and initiatives from scratch. This was particularly critical, due to a third issue. Since CEO's first formation, the support landscape for creative industries had grown considerably, becoming more complex and more competitive.

Our period of observation was marked by a number of strategic shifts designed to fit the organisation for the future, and these changes were accompanied by a significant amount of self-aware reflection, partly facilitated and certainly amplified by our presence as a research team. The outcome of this process can be seen within the *Business plan* produced by CEO in July 2014.[3] Orientated towards securing an increased Creative Scotland award, this provided a critical but positive stocktaking of the organisation's position and set out a number of ambitious new priorities and directions for its second decade of operation. Central to this was the interconnected rethinking of service delivery models, geographic reach and funding mix, involving changing the physical and digital mix of client support and developing a new 'Cascade' scheme for delivering workshops in partnership with local councils. The scoping of the new digital plans, the commissioning of a new website, and the piloting of Cascade had been facilitated by the award of £244,000 under Creative Scotland's Cultural Economy Fund for Infrastructure and Capacity Building. In addition, the organisation had begun to engage more deeply with research in order to engage in sector advocacy and was seeking to build an international consultancy profile.

Certain more administrative changes were also foregrounded within the *Business plan*, including a major restructuring of the organisation that

DOI: 10.1057/9781137478887.0008

we had observed during the summer of 2013. This consisted of a move to a less hierarchical, so-called podular system, posited by management as a means to improve organisational flexibility and enable CEO to cope with both the diversity of current activities and the inevitability of further change in the future. It was accompanied by the development of plans for a somewhat overdue overhaul of both CEO's internal Client Record Management (CRM) database and its outward-facing website, a particularly difficult process due to the conflict between the constraints posed by the limited funds available and the acute necessity of effecting ambitious change if CEO were to survive.

Given its centrality to the organisation's effective future functioning, this chapter also explores the changing role of data management and evidence gathering in a cultural intermediary such as CEO. This encompasses both the routine collection and circulation of data and the development of a one-off in-house research project which was led by the Chair of the Board, Bob Last. This leads us to consider how the formal management of knowledge enabled and shaped CEO's work.

In this chapter, we also wish to consider CEO's organisational ethos and management style. Whereas Chapters 3 and 4 addressed how the agency's services, belief-system and client interactions have been a product of thirteen years of incremental evolution, here we seek to reflect on the ways in which this history has shaped its internal organisational dynamics. How has CEO's trajectory to date enabled or impeded its ability to evolve?

Organisational restructuring

In the summer of 2013, CEO was restructured in line with the current trend in the creative sector for 'lean' organisations – that is, those that are small-scale, efficient, dynamic and flexible.[4] The new form mooted by the Director was designed to do away with the hierarchical and rigid structure that had developed as CEO had grown from a staff of three to nineteen. This was coupled, as mentioned in Chapter 4, with a decision to train all of the staff as accredited coaches, through an external training company, Relational Dynamics 1st. Both the structural shift and the organisation-wide staff training were envisaged by the Director as means to empower individual staff members, strengthen the team, and build organisational resilience. However, as the staff were not consulted about

DOI: 10.1057/9781137478887.0008

either development, and success depended on support at all levels of the organisation, this was potentially a high-risk strategy.

The existing organisational structure had allowed CEO to adapt to a number of changes in its external environment, while at the same time protecting CEO's core services. However, it could at best be described as ad hoc; it was assembled on an 'as-and-when' basis, with new staff hired and teams created in order to administer new projects and solve pressing problems. As a result of this demand-led expansion, the old structure suffered from an inherent lack of flexibility.

The new structure unveiled by the Director at a June 2013 staff meeting, was adapted from David Grey and Thomas Vander Wal's pop-management text, *The connected company*.[5] The Director's announcement was designed to be performative – that is, the 'new' structure was to come into existence with immediate effect.[6] However, in practice immediate change proved nearly impossible to implement. Interviews that we conducted with CEO staff during the summer and autumn of 2013 confirmed that they had not been consulted about the restructuring. This raised two questions for us. First, how and why had this particular approach been chosen? Second, what were the logic and ethos of the new structure and what impact would it have across the organisation?

In an interview, Deborah Keogh explained her selection of the new organisational model as serendipitous. She had been seeking to revise the organisation along less hierarchical lines and a consultant specialising in 'business transformation' and technology had suggested podular structures as a current trend. Although noting that she had initially been a little sceptical, on reading the book concerned, Keogh began to see its relevance for CEO's context and possibilities to adapt this new approach to her agency's advantage.[7]

Grey and Vander Wal note that as service companies grow, and become more complex, they may become disconnected from their clients. They contend that organisations must build enduring yet flexible relationships with their clients, stating that 'services introduce customers into operations, which creates complexity and variability that is hard to plan for in advance. Companies must find ways to accommodate variety at the edge of the organization, where people and systems interact directly with customers, partners, and suppliers'.[8]

In order for organisations to manage the variety in their client base, Grey and Vander Wal argue that there are clear advantages to what they term 'holarchies'; these are organisational structures where individual

DOI: 10.1057/9781137478887.0008

work units (called 'pods') can function both independently and as part of a whole. Grey and Vander Wal argue that 'podular' systems are better suited to customer-facing organisations, stating that 'a connected company learns and adapts by distributing control to the points of interaction with customers'.[9]

In the context of the challenges facing CEO, the Director presented the podular system to the staff partly as a means to resolve practical administrative problems such as urgent budget authorisation. However, it was also introduced as a potential means to address bottlenecks of expertise and information in the wider organisational culture. As noted in Chapter 4, when we conducted our interviews with CEO staff, it was clear that those individuals in customer-facing positions did not always feel able to make decisions independently; rather, they were also encouraged to 'refer up' wherever possible. This put strain on the in-house advisers, because clients would often be referred to them for an advice session when their enquiry could in fact be dealt with by one of the Business Support team on the phone, or via email. Instead, Business Support staff would often liaise with colleagues and senior managers before proceeding with client enquiries. The podular structure, in combination with the new company-wide coaching training, offered all the staff the potential to address this issue by enabling confident decision making at the point of client interaction.

However, while the podular structure was presented in terms of a number of clearly perceived potential gains, there were also some less visible risks. For example, it was unclear as to whether a podular structure might not in fact magnify the potential for organisational inefficiencies, by privileging autonomy over co-operation and collaboration. The research team also thought that pods might become 'siloes', and that staff, resources and ideas might become isolated due to the workings of the podular system. Additionally, from Grey and Vander Wal's text, it is not clear just how much hierarchy is appropriate for a 'connected company' or to what extent podularity truly represents a genuine departure from older organisational models that privilege hierarchy and functional divisions.

In the months after the new structure was mooted, the existing structure proved difficult to dislodge. In part, this was because the precise ways in which the change of structure would work were not clear and senior managers had not been given time to prepare their teams for the shift. Moreover, arguably, there was 'change fatigue'[10] among the staff

DOI: 10.1057/9781137478887.0008

more widely. In Chapter 3, we outlined CEO's operational history, noting that the most recent phase had entailed a considerable and rapid change: CEO moved to a new office, applied to become a charity, restructured its working teams, and commissioned a new CRM and website. However, the precarious, project-based nature of CEO's development meant that it lacked some of the standard features of a larger organisational infrastructure that would normally be key to the smooth management of change. In particular, human resources expertise was provided on a part-time, freelance basis and not fully integrated into the organisation, and there was no one with formal responsibility for managing internal and external corporate communications. If effectively used, such functions may help to ensure that staff are committed to an organisation, remain properly informed about plans and are thus able to be ambitious about its future.

During observation in 2013, it was clear that the pace of change had created challenges for staff at all levels. Many felt as if big decisions about the future were being made without consultation or sufficient explanation to enable them feel confident and comfortable with the changes. Due to external uncertainties regarding securing CEO's finances, senior management needed to keep certain key developments behind closed doors, but the move to an open-plan office made the discreet management of information difficult.

In recent years, a large body of academic literature has grown up concerning the management of organisational change. Change remains one of the most difficult facets of organisational life to plan for, manage, and evaluate, particularly if staff do not feel consulted about or properly prepared for it.[11] As already noted, due to its somewhat precarious position within the sector, much of the Director's time was taken up with securing funding and repositioning CEO in relation to new priorities within the creative economy, often moving rapidly in response to confidential information. As a result she could not always be as transparent about developments as might be ideal.

In this context, our one-to-one interviews and knowledge-exchange events created spaces where concerns and frustrations could be confidentially expressed. And to a limited degree, we acted as a kind of back channel, feeding impressions and contentious issues (suitably anonymised) back into the management process. CEO evidently saw continued benefit in including external perspectives in the change process. After we left the field, the Director brought in an external consultant, Sarah Thelwall, to facilitate the preparation of the *Business plan* and

DOI: 10.1057/9781137478887.0008

this appeared to have been a very positive and productive experience, creating – at least at management level – a clearer sense of direction and purpose in the articulation of the three-year plan. It was followed by the commissioning of a report by Social Value Lab, published in early 2015, to which we have already referred.

Re-imagining reach and service delivery

Thelwall's draft of the *Business plan* was unequivocal about the challenging future faced by the organisation:

> CEO has stretched its old model to a point where the drive for internal efficiency to support more clients has hampered the ability of the team to meet the clients' needs sufficiently quickly. The agility of a small organisation has been lost amongst the need to demonstrate to funders the value that is being delivered.[12]

As noted in the introduction to this chapter, CEO was overstretched. The organisation was forced to take stock of the changing support landscape, both in terms of its perceptions of changing client competences as well as the fact that there were now a number of other organisations offering effective services to businesses in the creative sector across Scotland. While CEO was still delivering the largest volume of support,[13] the larger mainstream business support agencies had become better at talking to creatives, with Business Gateway cited as helpful by many clients, and Scottish Enterprise increasingly committed to training and accrediting all of its business advisers in what has been for some time CEO's specialism, namely, coaching techniques.[14]

After 2008 a range of smaller, more nimble creative sector-focused initiatives sprang up around Scotland, in part influenced and shaped by CEO's work. Some of these were far flung, providing support in areas that CEO had never managed to reach. Emergents, in Inverness, has provided mentoring and business support in the Highlands, with a particular focus on crafts and writing. Social enterprise Eigg Box (on the Isle of Eigg) has supplied space and training to locals and creative sector visitors. Others overlapped with areas that CEO had covered since the Four Cities expansion. Both Creative Dundee and Creative Edinburgh had been run by people who had worked with or for CEO in the past, and in common with the more recent addition, Creative Stirling, they

DOI: 10.1057/9781137478887.0008

offered a combination of signposting to existing support sector provision and locally-focused creative community building through networking events.

The mode of address of these organisations was less formal than CEO's and they were more open to using their websites to promote members' work. A 2014 review by the consultancy EKOS, commissioned by Creative Scotland, concluded that one wider lesson to be drawn from these initiatives was that 'networks should be led and owned by the sector itself and not developed by the public sector on behalf of the creative community – the bottom-up approach has proved its value'.[15] The small scale and local responsiveness with which CEO had begun, was rediscovered as a merit.[16] It was clear to us that without decisive action to address such new developments, CEO was in danger of being left behind.

Scotland's sprawling geography and the rural location of many artists and makers have always magnified the challenge of providing access to services to all. Therefore, a key aspect of rethinking reach and delivery was through Cascade: a plan to licence workshops for delivery by local authority partners. This was driven by two factors: the realisation that the organisation could not expand its direct delivery any further, and pressure from the Scottish Government to diversify the organisation's business model and become less dependent on Creative Scotland funding.

Cascade ran from 2014 to 2015, funded as a 'capacity building' pilot project under the Sustainable Development Fund. This involved working with local partners to deliver four tried and tested workshops in the first instance, but with scope to develop further collaborative content and support advising in the future. The initial partners were the Scottish Borders' Creative Arts Business Network (CABN), Dumfries and Galloway Council and Fife Cultural Trust, reflecting both local authority commitments to the 'promotion of the creative industries sector as an area of ongoing growth and development',[17] and an increasing trend towards buying in some cultural services, as part of a drive to be more businesslike.

Defining how Cascade might work was a challenge for CEO. It meant that the agency needed to reflect on the nature of its IP, whether for instance this resided in its course materials or its organisational ethos and delivery style, and whether these could be packaged for delivery by others. Due to concerns about possible negative impacts on the CEO brand, initially, a franchise model was mooted, with CEO retaining

DOI: 10.1057/9781137478887.0008

tight control over the delivery and a desire to be closely involved in the recruitment and training of staff. However, over the course of the year, these initial requirements were relaxed. Cascade was launched with a content licence in place, allowing scope to tailor the course content to local need. Plans were also developed to set up a network for the new partner providers, sharing experiences, feeding back and enabling peer-to-peer support.

CEO's *Business plan* contained a clear acknowledgment that the current model, where increased demand was seen as reducing the resources available to clients, was no longer tenable.[18] In response to this, a key aspect of the 2015–2018 strategy hinged on making a significant investment in its digital platforms and web profile in order to reverse the balance of its delivery model from 80/20 physical/digital to 20/80 physical/digital. The proposed new model was ambitious, combining client-side inputs to the database with CEO-managed peer-to-peer mechanisms, all of which was intended to support a redefinition of the CEO-client relationship. This was described as 'a shift from servicing to enabling', meaning that 'the client actively leads the journey rather than being led by CEO' and potentially would begin to 'pay' for the support they received in kind, through their contributions to the peer network.[19] In October 2014, CEO launched the first phase of their new website, still purely information based rather than interactive but now offering a streamlined and less visually cluttered version of the old content. Phase two, the portal planned for late 2015, however, was dropped due to the failure to secure further funding. It remains pertinent, nonetheless, to reflect on the distance travelled by CEO in reimagining the IT infrastructure and the digital offer, the process this involved and the obstacles faced along the way.

Addressing IT systems and processes

The fundamental rethinking of the place of IT in service delivery outlined above is a long way from the more functional IT update mooted and scoped during our observations in the summer of 2013. Here, we wish to explore the reasons why. One of the greatest challenges of operating on a recurrent, short-term financial basis is that it makes it very difficult to prioritise long-term infrastructural planning and justify major investments in areas such as IT. Once, this just meant getting by with older

DOI: 10.1057/9781137478887.0008

computer hardware and obsolescent administrative software – something that could be patched up with a make-do-and-mend attitude.

However, the shift that has taken place online since 1999, from a static publishing model that has retrospectively come to be understood as Web 1.0 to the interactive, highly participatory environment of Web 2.0, has transformed (and continues to transform) our expectations of the online experience. E-commerce platforms have trained us to expect portals offering seamless personalised services. Social media mean we now routinely curate our own online presences on third-party sites, and interact with each other in informal and fluid ways. In this context, continuing digital investment is central to perceptions of good service delivery and a failure to keep up is hyper-visible, potentially jeopardising both reputation and market position. For CEO – which entered the field shortly after the cooling effects of the dot.com crash of 2000 and always used its website strictly in a push capacity, as an information repository, news feed and branding tool – this meant completely rethinking the way its online presence functioned, as well as the way it might manage both digital interactions with clients and the increasingly overburdened customer-facing services.

One of the biggest practical obstacles to imagining, let alone achieving, the proposed 80/20 split had been the way in which work routines based on the current IT systems were deeply embedded in office rhythms, established patterns and staff roles. The combined CRM database and web-content management system first designed in 2006 had had three major updates, partly driven by the fact that the addition of new programmes necessitated a number of bolt-ons. However, these upgrades were always limited to stretching and adapting the existing set-up to meet pressing needs, due to the absence of in-house IT expertise or funds that could be earmarked for periodic review and investment. Consequently, there was also a deficiency in information and training.

As noted, in late 2012, CEO submitted a Cultural Economy Sustainable Development funding bid to Creative Scotland. A significant portion was earmarked as an investment in IT Development and Infrastructure Costs, with separate amounts designated for the major CRM update, for a new website and the migration of existing content, and for the review and development process necessary to find a solution that fitted the bill. The latter aspect involved bringing in freelance IT and web consultants to help define what was needed, to scope possible options and devise the tender documentation that would form the basis of the contracts.

DOI: 10.1057/9781137478887.0008

However, these consulting jobs necessarily needed to take place – and partly be paid for – before the major investment was set in train and, although the bid was successful, a delay in releasing the money resulted in the timescales shifting. A further complication was that CEO was in the process of applying for charitable status at the time (a process then expected to be successful but subsequently abandoned in late 2014, after the funding cut). Due to the different scales charged to commercial and charity clients for proprietary software, the failure to become a charity radically changed how ambitious the plans could be.

Observing the work undertaken by the consultants hired to address CEO's IT needs, it became clear that their one-to-one interviews and group sessions with staff had built upon our own research. The consultants attempted to create a space in which staff could begin to articulate not just the ways in which the system did not work but also how it ought to. The pitches made and the interviews with those bidding for the work then further expanded management thinking about the desirable and the possible. Ultimately, stages that were ostensibly part of a tendering and commissioning process revealed the need for further consultation and consideration. Thus, the work undertaken with external consultants to define the tender briefs and the process of selecting and hearing pitches from potential service providers did not result in the outright commissioning of new systems on the timescale planned. Instead, it allowed CEO to understand its own strategic needs, learn about current options and begin to reimagine its future. In an ideal scenario, more time would have been built into these stages, with the planning preceding and informing the pitch for the money needed to commission and implement the new systems.

CEO's tentativeness in imagining its digital future needs to be understood in light of its precariousness and the profound effects this had on organisational thinking. An acute consciousness of financial limitations and an ingrained culture of make-do-and-mend at every level meant that staff made a virtue out of their ability to circumnavigate their less than ideal system, neither hoping nor pushing for the level of IT development that they clearly felt was essential to CEO's ability to remain up to date and competitive. As the funds that would have enabled them to push their more ambitious plans forward did not ultimately materialise, this underscored the need pragmatically to stay within limited horizons. However, in the longer-term, this could only have crippling effects.

DOI: 10.1057/9781137478887.0008

Generating the evidence, making the case

When we began researching CEO, it became clear that the Client Record Management database was extremely important to the organisation. On the one hand, it was absolutely central as a practical tool, used daily to navigate client histories and make bookings and periodically to collate data for reporting purposes. On the other, it had a more symbolic value. Particularly for longer-serving members of management, it was understood as a cumulative and inherently valuable repository of knowledge, the digital trace of over a decade's worth of client interactions – a possible resource to mobilise and tell different kinds of stories about the organisation and its clients. Providing evidence of impact is a constant concern for all publicly-funded bodies charged with making interventions. CEO's claim to usefulness has been based on knowing the creative sector better than other types of business support agency. However, it did not have the systems in place in order to collate, curate and mobilise this knowledge, thereby enhancing its future performance.

There is a tension between the need to provide evidence for service delivery according to the criteria set out by funders, and alternatively, the desire to build a body of evidence that might inform future policy agendas. By way of example, CEO has argued for the sustainability of creative businesses to be taken as seriously as their growth potential. This view was rooted in a specific understanding of the creative sector. It was a counterpoint to a mainstream business support culture that has tended to characterise the micro-business as merely a passing phase for an enterprise that – as a criterion of success – should at least aim to grow into an SME.

Had it received funding to establish the proposed new portal, CEO would have been able to gather extensive new client data. However, it would still have faced the major challenge of making its new capacity work as a strategic tool for sector research and advocacy. This would certainly have depended on developing at least some research capability.

Research and advocacy

Following the appointment of a board in 2009, CEO began to seek a more active advocacy role within the sector and policy. Its *Business plan*

DOI: 10.1057/9781137478887.0008

indicated that the development of more research and advocacy was a goal. For example, two key objectives were set out as follows:

> Capture and analyse client data and sector intelligence to inform the production of relevant content and events, addressing the business development needs of the sector.

> Establish a pool of Industry Associates who can work with CEO to establish a think tank and publishing arm, to produce provocative and insightful content with a perspective on macro conditions leading to annual strategic facing events and seminars.[20]

There is substance in these recommendations but they would need the right conditions to enable them to be put into effect. To illustrate this point, there are relevant lessons to be learned from a research project conducted under the auspices of CEO during the period of our study.

When we began this study, some related work was being conducted by Bob Last, then Chair of CEO's Board, who had produced a discussion paper titled *Creative Industries in Scotland: micro-businesses, access to finance and the public purse*, in March 2012.[21] Following a meeting with the Scottish Government to discuss his thinking, a research project was commissioned to start on 1 April 2013, run through CEO. Its remit was to investigate 'Creative micro-businesses and access to finance'.

Prior to the launch of that project, Last's paper was circulated to several individuals from whom comments were invited. Philip Schlesinger, one of those consulted about the initial think piece, was invited to join the project's steering group, along with David Cook, then Chief Executive of WASPS and a former CEO Board member, Roanne Dods, Director of Performing Arts Labs, and Clive Gillman, Director of Dundee Contemporary Arts.[22] Diane Campion, a senior policy adviser for broadcasting and the creative industries in the Culture Division of the Scottish Government, joined the advisory group as project sponsor. The steering group first met on 4 July 2013, at CEO's offices. Deborah Keogh was in the chair.

The project's brief was to address 'the barriers to financing creative sector micro-businesses and thoughts on an appropriate government response to mitigating these'.[23] Micro-businesses were defined in terms of the EU's approach as 'having less than ten employees and turnover of less than 2 million Euros'.[24] The research would 'present an articulation of the ecological make up of the sector and how, if demonstrated, its characteristics differ from other sectors'.

DOI: 10.1057/9781137478887.0008

The project was initially intended to run from 1 April to 31 October 2013, but as Last's views developed in the light of his emerging findings, his interpretation of the material became increasingly complex and his aims more sophisticated and ambitious. The project overran the original short time-scale, finally reporting in October 2014. The report, however, did not see the light of day until well into 2015, when it was finally submitted to the Scottish Government.[25]

According to the project brief, the eventual report was intended to aim at 'wider consideration by policy makers, public sector funders and investors'. It would seek to review what was known about the extent of the creative industries in Scotland,[26] identify 12–15 interviewees across different sectors to assess their motivations and subsequently go into further depth to produce case studies. The research would also set out to develop 'financial models', devise a matrix to map 'value and performance' and also the 'support and advice structures' that might be needed.[27] Interestingly, and tellingly, the latter more quantitative measures, much beloved by governments, did not find their way into the final report, given the study's evolution.

As a first step, Bob Last identified 13 interviewees who worked in games, publishing, visual arts, music, jewellery, design, architecture and fashion, as well as one major business sponsor of the arts. The informants ranged across highly successful businesses (including a Turner Prize winner), well-established enterprises, and creative workers with emerging reputations but who were making a precarious living. To construct this sample, Last had identified 'a cross section of art forms and business types' from 'those at very early stages to the more mature, those who had engaged with public support and those who had not'.[28]

Bob Last's interviews were detailed qualitative explorations of his subjects' working lives, the cultural values they espoused, and how these fitted into making a living as well as their wider ambitions – both professional and social. The steering group advised Last and CEO that the project should not be driven 'by narrow economic calculation' and hoped that it would be a 'trigger for policy development'.[29] There was an undoubted tension between the needs of the Scottish Government for policy advice constructed in conventionally recognisable terms and the contrary view that this research could be a way to explore new directions.

By the time the steering committee first met, Last had identified emergent themes, including relationships between opportunities and risks,

DOI: 10.1057/9781137478887.0008

the wider cultural context for creative work, how material and critical success might lead to less – but higher value – production, and also the economic fragility of apparently successful businesses that are nonetheless reaching international markets.[30] It was decided that at the midpoint the project would aim to explore further the economics of businesses at a fairly early stage of development, the better to understand the challenges faced. To that end a detailed questionnaire was devised.

After its second meeting on 21 August 2013, the steering committee did not reconvene. The Scottish Government's project sponsor moved on and other issues crowded in, which meant that the research lost momentum. By this stage, Bob Last and Deborah Keogh were engaged in protracted negotiations about CEO's future funding and scope of activity with the Scottish Government and Creative Scotland. At one tense Board meeting on 30 September 2013, deeply frustrated by a failure to make progress regarding CEO's role and funding with the Scottish Government, Last made it clear that he wished to step down from chairing CEO, not immediately but certainly in the foreseeable future.

Indeed, by the time the project had neared completion, Bob Last had stepped down from chairing CEO's Board, which he did in April 2014, completing five years' service. There was some behind-the-scenes discussion about the focus and scope of the research before Deborah Keogh finally sent a draft to the steering committee for comment on 4 July 2014. Last sent out a revised version to the steering committee on 17 August 2014. The complete package finally submitted to the Scottish Government consisted of the report, transcripts of the interviews, case studies of the financial aspects of six of the cases, and Dr Inge Sørensen's literature review.

The lengthy gestation of this piece of work meant that it had moved away from focusing on financial intervention into creative micro-businesses, shifting instead into reflections on the values adopted by creatives and how these played into their place within a 'cultural economy'. The new title indicated the shift: *Creativity, value and money*. The paper's first part involved reflections on policy, evidence and the nature of creativity. It then addressed several themes mostly by presenting extracts from the interviews, before concluding with reflections on policy challenges. In appearance, it certainly looked neither like a conventional consultant's report nor an academic paper but rather like an extended, somewhat literary, reflective essay, which from a practical point of view raised some intriguing questions about its likely reception in official circles.

DOI: 10.1057/9781137478887.0008

In an email to the steering committee when he delivered his draft, Bob Last wrote:

> You will note that the paper closes with a set of policy challenges rather than a specific policy proposal – this is because on reflection I take the view that what the paper suggests in terms of my own thinking but more importantly in terms of the thinking and practice present in the interviews is that the overwhelming value for policy would be to engage with a rethink of the understanding of the creative industries and how to engage with them. I would argue this is the strongest and most useful message from the work and that, in essence, current structures and understandings are not an adequate basis for new effective and efficient policy initiatives.
>
> I also suggest that in posing policy challenges the paper can possibly be usefully used for further debate.[31]

This was a clear steer as to how the work should be interpreted, recognising that it presents a challenge to the conventional wisdom. To illustrate why, we shall draw out some of Last's key points.

First, rather than assume that creative work is all about the pursuit of exploitable IP by an individualistic competitive agent, Last suggests instead that it concerns

> the active sharing of [...] intangible values [...] creating a collective capital [...] that is open-source in nature, that thrives in the public domain, that is a source of validation for the contributor and that can be drawn on by all and, of especial note, is free to use for start ups.[32]

Second, addressing the Scottish Government, Last takes issue with the very idea of the creative industries, asking what a non-creative one might look like,[33] and argues that policy-making risks being too simplistic in the creative industries field as it needs better alignment 'with the goals and values of those it seeks to impact'.[34] Third, he argues – in common with much of the literature, and doubtless influenced by his own direct experience – that creative enterprises are distinct from 'more conventional commercial endeavours' because 'the whole of a person or proprietors (sic) value system and life is engaged or invested in the business'.[35] This, he goes on to suggest, is connected to a characteristic of creative products, their special or 'meta' value – in essence their capacity (over and beyond the process in which they are produced) to engender emotional effects, notably pleasure.[36] Last concludes by raising questions about the ability of current official categories to capture the nature and extent of the creative industries, proposing that the best way forward is to take

DOI: 10.1057/9781137478887.0008

a soft funding approach to imaginative ventures that will contribute to 'collective cultural capital' and thereby enrich society and underpin a common resource. He notes that this does not conform to current practice, not least that in Creative Scotland.

These are not the usual terms in which governments, civil servants and funders are addressed and without further facilitating intervention to ensure that the ideas are discussed and tested, it seems likely that they will either not be understood or fall on deaf ears.

One question that arose during our fieldwork was whether CEO could develop a standing research capacity. Bob Last's work on the conditions of creative enterprise showed that interesting and challenging research could be produced from within an agency such as CEO. The work in question owed much to the personal characteristics of the researcher, however, and would not classify either as academic research or as consultancy. What Last also showed – which again was specific to his own approach, supported by his steering committee – is that a project can be fruitfully redefined in the process of investigation, whatever the brief, although how that affects its eventual reception is another matter. The case also showed that it is possible to mobilise expert external advice on a pro bono basis to support such ventures. Furthermore, it also proved possible to sub-contract more peripheral aspects of the research process – such as the review of the grey literature – by bringing in appropriate academic or other skilled expertise.

All of that said, for the academic analyst accustomed to a different work regime with much more detailed project management and strict reporting deadlines in play, it is striking how difficult it was for CEO to manage the research process to ensure a timely outcome, not least when the researcher in question was a busy and prominent filmmaker, internationally connected, and a public figure in Scotland. This implies both that a suitable structure would need to be put in place if bodies such as CEO were to add research to their portfolios, and moreover, that if such work were to be done routinely, there would have to be trained capacity in the organisation both to undertake the research and also to manage it.

But it was not just the absence of a sustaining research management system that affected the process. The research was under way at a time when CEO was deeply engaged in addressing its future funding in a dialogue with its paymasters. Last's major involvement in this process, along with his day-to-day commitments, added a further disruptive effect to the smooth conduct of the research. We might surmise that the delay in publication was at least in part due to concern inside CEO about its possible adverse effects on funding. While contingencies commonly do affect research projects, protections do need to be place to ensure that they stay on course. As noted, Last's research was challenging in its approach and conclusions, although it is too early to know what its impact – if any – will be.[37]

Conclusion

CEO's history and current context have shaped and constrained its infrastructure, planning ability and management style. Its gradual but always uncertain journey from a series of finite projects to an established organisation meant that some of the standard elements of a larger infra-structure were not developed, in particular HR, investment in commu-nications and IT, and long-term planning.

The last phase of our research was deeply shaped by the funding crisis into which CEO was pitched by the reduction in its grant in late 2014. This had a profound effect on its plans. In this chapter, we have indicated the kinds of direction in which the management had planned to move. These included a major overhaul of the IT system and, linked to this, a radical rethinking of the relationship with the client base. These ambi-tious changes in strategy were premised on CEO keeping its present staffing base. The reduction in funding made it impossible to sustain the operation at that level.

As we have seen, with an eye to reshaping its internal workings, the agency had engaged in a major restructuring process, shifting from a hierarchical system to one based on 'podularity'. The Director opted to reform the organisation without full consultation with the staff and it took some time for the new set-up to establish itself. Although these changes did not involve extensive preparation, by contrast, detailed steps were taken to prepare the ground for the new IT system. But a lack of resources meant that this could not be implemented as intended.

There were also plans in train to develop research. This was connected to the Chair of the Board and Director's wish to develop a distinctive approach to the creative industries and to enter into the debate about the future shape of the support agencies – in effect, making CEO into a player. The attempt to gain ground in the policy debate failed and

DOI: 10.1057/9781137478887.0008

resulted first, in the resignation of the Chair and then, after attempts to work within CEO's adverse funding position, the eventual decision to move on by the Director on 20 February 2015.

A key pressure at the centre of all of these developments has been the need to work in a more businesslike way in order to ensure an efficient and secure long-term future for CEO. This means adopting the mantle of an organisation operating compliantly within the *realpolitik* of the ideologically over-determined policy landscape outlined in Chapter 2. To some extent such connivance cuts across the desire to work more strategically on behalf of the sector to change radically the terms of the conversation about creative micro-businesses and, given sufficient clarity, to intervene in policy.

The pressure on CEO has been for it to be an efficient, proactive and cost-effective agent of policy delivery, and crucially, to be perceived as such at Scottish Government level and by Creative Scotland, the joint means by which public funding for the creative sector is distributed. This means embracing the existing rhetoric on the creative economy and visibly embodying its objectives while also carefully negotiating any discrepancies in priorities that might arise between the Scottish Government and Creative Scotland's management. Moreover, even this approach offers no guarantees. Plainly, an organisation such CEO remains vulnerable to shifts of priorities by its funding bodies, and sometimes no amount of trying to read the runes will help.

This unpredictability and its adverse consequences is reflected in the highly revealing statement given to us by Deborah Keogh following her departure from CEO, just as this book went to press:

> With great difficulty, I decided it was time to move on. In the end, I felt that it was the only positive thing left to do. With seriously big cuts coming from Creative Scotland, and no space for adult dialogue or inventive alternative planning, I could not see a way to deliver a version of the services with the same quality, expertise and flexibility that we had become known and trusted for. It is my sincere hope that someone new with a different perspective will be able to move things on in a new way. This has been a huge disappointment and is deeply ironic, that after years of solid work with a broad group of economic development stakeholders, raising awareness of the value and effectiveness of expert support, that it was in the end the agency whose policy it is to provide these services that withdrew funding. In the absence of any other current strategy for creative industries, and following an absolutely glowing independent review of CEO, this seems rather short sighted.

DOI: 10.1057/9781137478887.0008

In the short time I have had to reflect since moving on, it seems to me that the role of the intermediary is an incredibly complex one, set up to address a gap in provision, or market failure, something it proves beyond doubt is required and then is expected to operate more like a commercial organisation while in the solid pursuit of its mission.

I also wonder how much more effective CEO could have been if it had been initially set up as a 10-year project, to effect a change in the landscape and was given proper funding to do it. All the time wasted in raising more money, in convincing new leadership about the evolution of things and the history, could have just gone into the highest quality delivery of expertise to our creatives, to help them on their way. After all, that is what the job we undertook was all about. It was never about empire building. But as soon as you are thrown into fighting for your survival as an entity, the actual work that you do gets sidelined.[38]

Notes

1   'Frequently asked questions', Creative Scotland, accessed 10 March 2015, http://www.creativescotland.com/contact-us/enquiries/funding/regular-funding/post-application-faqs/in-the-main-sector-support-organisations-are-not-being-included-as-part-of-the-new-portfolio-what-is-the-reasoning-behind-this-decision.

2   'Annual clients 2014/15', Creative Scotland, accessed 10 March 2015, http://www.creativescotland.com/funding/latest-information/funded-organisations/annual-clients.

3   Cultural Enterprise Office, *Cultural Enterprise Office business plan 2015–2018* (Glasgow: Cultural Enterprise Office, 2014).

4   'What is Lean?'

5   David Grey and Thomas Vander Wal, *The connected company* (Sebastopol, CA: O'Reilly Media, 2012).

6   Two members of the research team, Ealasaid Munro and Melanie Selfe, were present at the meeting and learned about the restructure at the same time as the majority of the staff.

7   Interview with Deborah Keogh, 1 June 2014.

8   Grey and Vander Wal, *The connected company*, v.

9   Ibid., vii.

10   Patrick Dawson, *Understanding organizational change: the contemporary experience of people at work* (London: Sage, 2003), 168.

11   Ibid., 168.

12   Cultural Enterprise Office, *Business plan 2015–2018*, 16.

DOI: 10.1057/9781137478887.0008

13   Alan McGregor, *Cultural economy support research: final report [revised draft November 2012]* (Glasgow: University of Glasgow Training & Employment Research Unit, 2012).

14   'Premier Advisor, SFEDI Diploma in Business and Enterprise Support', Academy of Leadership and Management, accessed 10 March 2015, http://www.academylm.co.uk/courses/premier-advisor/.

15   EKOS, *Summary of EKOS mapping review of three creative city networks: report prepared for Creative Scotland* (Glasgow: EKOS, 2014), 1–3.

16   However, the other creative city networks have also encountered demands to provide better evidence of their effectiveness, and have recently found their access to Creative Scotland support restricted.

17   The Scottish Government, *Support for creative industries: roles and responsibilities, briefing 5 February 2009* (Edinburgh: The Scottish Government, 2009).

18   Cultural Enterprise Office, *Cultural Enterprise Office business plan 2015–2018*, 16.

19   Ibid., 16.

20   Ibid., 23.

21   Bob Last, *Creative industries in Scotland: micro-businesses, access to finance and the public purse. Draft report prepared for Creative Scotland* (Glasgow: Cultural Enterprise Office, 2012).

22   Clive Gillman has been appointed Director of Creative Industries at Creative Scotland, with effect from June 2015.

23   Cultural Enterprise Office, *Project brief* (Glasgow: Cultural Enterprise Office, undated), np.

24   European Commission, *The new SME definition: user guide and model declaration* (Brussels: European Commission, 2005), 15.

25   Bob Last, *Creativity, value and money* (Glasgow: Cultural Enterprise Office, 2014).

26   This work was carried out by Dr Inge Sørensen, who had been appointed to a research fellowship at CCPR. She had not at that stage taken up her post at the Centre. This is an indication of just how closely CCPR was working in partnership with CEO. Dr Sørensen's original report was titled *Literature review of the definition, size and turnover of the creative industries and micro-businesses in Scotland: preliminary research*, May 2013. This was incorporated into part 2 of Bob Last's report, which contained his interviews and also secondary research.

27   Cultural Enterprise Office, *Project brief*, np.

28   Minutes, First meeting of the short-life steering group for the 'Creative micro businesses & access to finance research project', 4 July 2013, Philip Schlesinger's personal collection, np.

29   Ibid., np.

30   Ibid., np.

DOI: 10.1057/9781137478887.0008

31   Email from Bob Last to the steering group for the 'Creative micro businesses & access to finance research project', 8 July 2014, Philip Schlesinger's personal collection, np.

32   Last, *Creativity*, 7.

33   Ibid, 11.

34   Ibid, 9.

35   Ibid, 29.

36   Ibid, 30.

37   It is intended to hold a round-table at CCPR to discuss the work.

38   Email from Deborah Keogh, 25 March 2015, Philip Schlesinger's personal collection, np.

DOI: 10.1057/9781137478887.0008

6
Where Next for Cultural Business Support?

Abstract: *This chapter concludes the book. It argues that support for the creative economy now operates within a largely unchallenged set of assumptions. However, given that policy makers evidently think that bodies such as CEO are important for pursuing national goals, too little attention has been paid to their precarious conditions of existence. Our study has shown that, irrespective of contemporary political change, Scottish creative economy policy has remained highly dependent on UK initiatives and ideas. Moreover, the cross-border transfer of people and practices has also been important in establishing commonalities of approach. These, though, should not obscure the continuing importance, specificity and impact of place for the functioning of cultural business support, and not least the role of the local funding regime in shaping its periodically changing mission.*

Keywords: creative economy; cultural intermediaries; place; policy dependency; precariousness

Schlesinger, Philip, Melanie Selfe and Ealasaid Munro. *Curators of Cultural Enterprise: A Critical Analysis of a Creative Business Intermediary*. Basingstoke: Palgrave Macmillan, 2015. DOI: 10.1057/9781137478887.0009.

DOI: 10.1057/9781137478887.0009

This book has provided the first-ever detailed portrait of a neglected type of cultural intermediary that has become an inherent part of the creative economy: namely, the type of agency focused on ensuring that cultural micro-businesses have the skills to survive and thrive. Micro-businesses, rather than enterprises of significant scale, or even SMEs, are now the most characteristic way of organising contemporary creative work, so the work of such bodies is highly pertinent to the workings of the marketplace. Our case in this study – Cultural Enterprise Office – is therefore inherently revealing, not least as so little has been written about what goes on inside such bodies.

Tasked with making the creative sector business-like and efficient, cultural agencies' own conditions of existence have been largely ignored by policy-makers, consultants and most academics. Little attention has been paid to how organisations such as CEO work; and fundamental questions have not been posed. Do we need such intermediaries? Does it matter if they come and go? Could they possibly operate effectively without public subsidy in a state such as the UK? Could they add new, valuable knowledge to our understanding of precarious cultural work?

Provoked by this research, these are the kinds of questions that need to be asked in future work of this kind. However, they are hardly ever made explicit. Just as creative economy thinking has come to be a mostly unchallenged framework of beliefs, the broad nature of the required institutional order has also remained unquestioned. Of course, there is turbulence; fashions change, terms wax and wane, and support agencies come and go. A major case in point, for instance, of the latter was the rise and fall of the UK Film Council, created by a Labour government and axed by the Conservative-Liberal Democrat coalition.[1] Or, to take another example, we have witnessed the star-crossed trajectory of Creative Scotland, built on the ashes of its predecessors. Such organisational comings and goings are the norm. But they now occur within a support framework that has itself become normalised, that of the economisation of cultural life, and a deep-seated belief in the need for intervention in the interests of global competitiveness.

In this study, we have sought to strike a balance between describing and explaining the day-to-day activities of one typical organisation and demonstrating the wider import of our findings. In reflecting on what we have discovered, there are several key points to be made in conclusion.

First, at a time of major, and unresolved, change in the UK's politics and constitutional framework, our examination of CEO has much to

DOI: 10.1057/9781137478887.0009

tell about the relationship between British and Scottish policy-making with particular reference to cultural policy. In the wake of Scotland's referendum on independence and the coming redefinition of the scope of political devolution within the UK state, it remains the case that there is a considerable and unacknowledged level of dependency on UK policymakers in shaping the Scottish dimension of the creative economy. The uncritical adoption, in Scotland, of ideas minted in London during the heyday of New Labour – which, as we have pointed out, still rule the roost irrespective of changes of government at Westminster – means that the creative industries occupy a central place in Scotland's economic planning, despite the challenges posed to the idea of the 'creativity fix'[2] by the present economic crisis. The importance accorded to the income-generating potential of the creative economy is reflected in the current institutional apparatus. As has been pointed out, it was the deep policy dependency on policies developed in London that led directly to the birth of Creative Scotland,[3] the national body whose influence was continually evident in our research in CEO, most notably through the funding decisions taken and the expectations that these embodied.

As it stands, the idea of the creative economy is built upon at least two key assumptions: first, that it actually exists as an object for policy, and second, that intervention is a key way in which the component industries can be made more robust. In Scotland, as far as the creative economy is concerned, there has been no challenge to London's received wisdom. It has simply been adapted to local circumstance. This means that policymakers, cultural intermediary agencies, and creative practitioners themselves have yet to begin thinking differently about the relations between culture and the economy in the Scottish national context.

Our study has also highlighted the importance of influential third parties, in particular, NESTA. There has been a lack of academic attention regarding this body in recent years that is only now being remedied.[4] NESTA's influence has extended to government and policy makers, who have bought in to that body's focus on innovation. But far less apparent, has been NESTA's unobtrusive influence on cultural intermediary agencies at the coalface of cultural support. CEO has been an exemplary case of how this operates.

Alongside the movement of ideas via influential third parties such as NESTA, our research demonstrates that a further under-explored facet of policy mobility pertains to the movement of highly skilled individuals, and the quotidian practices that sustain the creative industries. The

DOI: 10.1057/9781137478887.0009

creative sector is characterised by the fluid movement of individuals between policy, consultancy, academia and intermediaries. For example, within Scotland, CEO is a particularly important node through which influential practitioners have passed.[5] Our study of CEO shows that, as these individuals move, they bring with them embodied knowledge about the creative economy, as well as programme templates, tools and modalities of working that all serve to further institutionalise the creative economy.

Second, despite the globalised nature of creative economy discourse, place undoubtedly still matters for research. Our study of CEO, and the particular economic, political and cultural milieu within which it operates has highlighted the need to understand cultural intermediaries in context – what works, what doesn't, and why. Our examination of CEO and its relationship with government, its principal funder, and its clients clearly demonstrates that there is no 'one size fits all' model for attempting to support the creative economy. Local circumstance and conditions continue to be of overwhelming importance. The rise and fall of CEO's Cardiff and Manchester counterparts, discussed elsewhere in this book, illustrate this clearly.

While this may be thought to be self-evident, it is nonetheless worth saying. Because despite targeted policy attention since devolution, Scotland's creative industries still struggle to compete with London. That is hardly surprising, given the widely recognised magnetic pull of the UK's capital city. Recent research by NESTA shows that employment growth in the creative sector stood at 4.3 per cent between 2011 and 2013, outstripping the average growth of the overall UK workforce.[6] However, 43 per cent of the UK's entire creative workforce is located in London and the South East, which means that these predominate as the centres for creative activity.[7] By contrast, employment in the Scottish creative economy fell by 1 per cent between 2011–2013, making Scotland the only region whose creative economy contracted at that time.[8] The argument for independence did not take Scotland's structural weakness in this domain into account, nor indeed really address the fact that London's lodestar status would have continued irrespective of constitutional change. Such recent statistics highlight the need to question whether business as usual is in any way appropriate for Scotland as a regional cultural economy.

A third key point we address in this book is the idea of 'success', insofar as it is applied to creative practitioners and their businesses. Our research

DOI: 10.1057/9781137478887.0009

into CEO calls into question policymakers' criteria for success, and how the 'health' and robustness of the creative economy are conventionally understood. Other authors have noted that the predominantly economic measures of success – business turnover, growth, sustainability – which prevail within policy discourse are often at odds with how creative practitioners themselves understand their work. Susan Luckman, for example, has suggested that, for creative practitioners, success might be as much about striking a happy work-life balance as increasing their profit margins.[9]

As we have shown, a key element of CEO's brand has been the specific kind of understanding its staff have brought to their engagement with clients. In many ways, this has set CEO apart from other intermediary organisations. The 'We are our clients' mentality so strongly apparent in many of the interactions that we witnessed stemmed directly from the fact that CEO's own position was also highly precarious. Many of CEO's staff were *au fait* with the need to build a portfolio career, with some supplementing their own continuing creative practice with other work. CEO, as we have demonstrated, had always been a precarious organisation, buffeted by the same policy winds as the clients it served. Crucially, recognising the conditions under which creative work is conducted led CEO to develop a holistic understanding of clients as individual creative practitioners with complex, messy and inherently unpredictable careers, rather than as discrete creative businesses. However, the dominant concern of government, policy-makers and third parties such as NESTA remains centred on the creative business.

Its focus on the individual, rather than the often fragile and fugitive business or businesses that any given individual might be affiliated with, has meant that CEO's model of support has offered a distinctive take on large swathes of the creative economy. To assess whether or not creative individuals are able to build a career in the creative industries requires a nuanced understanding of the conditions under which creative labour takes place. In this regard, our analysis accords with work being done elsewhere. Writing about the Australian context, Ruth Bridgstock has argued that overwhelmingly, the focus within creative industries support agencies is on sustainable businesses, when it might be better deployed in enabling sustainable individual careers in the creative industries.[10]

Our research suggests that one of the key barriers to creative practitioners seeking to build their career in the arts and creative industries in Scotland is the sheer complexity of the funding and support system.

DOI: 10.1057/9781137478887.0009

During the planning stages of Creative Scotland, the then Scottish Culture Minister, Mike Russell, proclaimed that there would be 'no wrong door for artists and creative practitioners seeking support'.[11] In actual fact, the proliferation of support agencies has led to frustration on the part of creative practitioners who often simply do not know where best to turn.

Our study of CEO has shown the difficulties faced by a small agency that has veered territorially between having a local presence in the city of Glasgow, achieving a wider multi-urban reach, and at moments seeking a yet-unattained ambition to have national scope. As we were undertaking fieldwork in CEO, Bob Last and Deborah Keogh were trying to renegotiate its place in the support landscape, both through advocacy and research. The existing institutional order proved to be too tough a nut to crack. At this time of writing, it remains the case that Scotland's agencies have overlapping or unclear remits and are without an overarching directive vision for how they should conduct their business.[12] Scotland is not unique. The complexity that characterises the intermediary landscape has been identified not only within the UK,[13] but also elsewhere, as creative economy policies have assumed greater importance in regional and national growth strategies.[14]

One of CEO's problems – which undoubtedly stood in the way of the ambitions pursued in 2013 – was how the proliferation of agencies led to a continuing competition for resources between intermediaries, as well as one between intermediaries and their clients. As Susan Jones has noted, the space occupied by intermediaries means creative practitioners find themselves at the end of a 'long food chain', increasingly distanced from policymakers.[15] Jones has examined the knock-on effects of the growth in number of intermediaries, emphasising that they are not only competing with each other but also with creative practitioners for ever-shrinking pots of money.

Rather than pose the usual question about how to judge the efficacy of intervention in the creative economy – about which we all know strikingly little – our study has considered the preconditions for intervention through intermediaries. Consequently, this is as much as anything a story of how a precariously-funded agency must typically look first and foremost to its own survival while adapting pragmatically to the prevailing winds of funders' whims as well as fashionable changes in terminology and practices. We have avoided the temptation of judging the overall merits of intervention, which was never our question. However, we would argue that as long as well-evidenced effectiveness remains the watchword for government, policy makers and other influential parties, the prevailing conditions for agencies such as CEO – which combine intense competition and extreme precariousness – make little sense. If intervention is going to remain central to governments' plans to grow the creative economy, then intermediaries require more stability so that they might develop more autonomously and have the scope to exploit their own knowledge of the sectors they are serving.

Finally, we wish to consider the role of academics in the constitution of the creative economy as an object of research and an increasingly elaborated discourse. Ours has been an Arts and Humanities Research Council-funded knowledge exchange project. In the UK in particular, there is increasing pressure on academics to engage with government and policymakers, industry, and the public, to ensure effective knowledge exchange between universities and the wider world, and demonstrate the useful impact of research beyond academia. If this is seen as a proper purpose to be pursued by the citizen-academic, that is one thing. It is certainly in this spirit that we engaged in exchanges with the staff of CEO during the course of our study, offering an outside view of their current practice on the one hand, and learning much about the functioning of a cultural intermediary on the other. However, if knowledge exchange ends up merely being a response to the imperatives of the state's audit culture and the purpose is simply to tick a box, then we would question its value. Likewise, Chris Gibson has emphasised that academics should turn a critical eye on the role that they themselves play in the performative constitution of the creative economy, and asked how they might articulate progressive alternatives.[16] We would certainly endorse that call to be reflexive and think afresh.

However, to date the impact of critical research on the creative economy policy juggernaut has been negligible.[17] Calls from critical academics to rethink the most fundamental assumptions regarding the creative economy have gone largely unheeded. That has not been our aim here. Rather, this study has sought to recognise the force of how the creative economy is presently imagined without thereby endorsing the dominant framework. Ironically, it is the current fixation on the creative economy that created the space for this work. By providing a detailed anatomy of a specific case, therefore, we have sought to show how that ideological framework of ideas is reproduced: embedded in policy, shaping institutions' priorities and inherent in the specific practices of

DOI: 10.1057/9781137478887.0009

a cultural intermediary such as CEO, it therefore sets the terms of trade for those engaged in cultural work. The challenge now is to think beyond those apparently compelling relations.

Notes

1   Doyle et al., *The rise and fall of the UK Film Council.*

2   Jakob and van Heur, 'Editorial: Taking matters into third hands', 357.

3   Philip Schlesinger, 'The politics of media and cultural policy', (Media@LSE working papers series, London School of Economics, 2009), www.lse.ac.uk/media@lse/research/mediaWorkingPapers/pdf/EWP17.pdf.

4   For a key exception see: Oakley et al., 'The national trust for talent?': 297.

5   Illustrating two such unnoticed pathways, Siân Prime worked for NESTA before setting up CEO and currently works at Goldsmiths University of London. Similarly, Lynsey Smith, instrumental in effecting the Starter for 6 handover, had previously worked at NESTA, moved to CEO to manage Starter for 6, moved again to set up Creative Edinburgh, and is currently at the British Council.

6   NESTA, *The geography of the UK's creative and high-tech economies*, 4–5.

7   Ibid., 5.

8   Ibid., 5; Rebecca Burns-Callender, 'Scotland's creative economy shrinks as London sucks out talent', *The Telegraph*, 28 January 2015, accessed 17 February 2015, http://www.telegraph.co.uk/finance/jobs/11372571/Scotlands-creative-economy-shrinks-as-London-sucks-out-talent.html.

9   Susan Luckman, *Locating cultural work: the politics and poetics of rural, regional and remote creativity* (London: Palgrave Macmillan, 2012).

10   Ruth Bridgstock, 'Making it creatively: building sustainable careers in the arts and creative industries', *Australian Career Practitioner Magazine* 22 (2011): 11–13.

11   Arts Professional, 'Scottish creative industries support', *Arts Professional*, 29 June 2009, accessed 27 February 2015, http://www.artsprofessional.co.uk/news/scottish-creative-industries-support.

12   A review – the outcome of which is still awaited – has been under way since spring 2014. Creative Scotland expects to publish it in 2015.

13   Tom Fleming, 'Targeting creativity through the intermediary: regional and local approaches in the UK and beyond', in *Creative industries and developing countries: voice, choice and economic growth*, ed. Diana Barrowclough and Zeljka Kozul-Wright (Abingdon: Routledge, 2008), 275.

14   Tara Vinodrai, 'Constructing the creative economy: design, intermediaries and institutions in Toronto and Copenhagen', *Regional Studies* 49 (2015): 275;

DOI: 10.1057/9781137478887.0009

Stefan Toepler, 'Shifting cultural policy landscapes in the USA: what role for philanthropic foundations?' *Cultural Trends* 22 (2013): 167.

15   Susan Jones, 'What are artists really worth? Funding, friction and the future of art', *The Guardian*, 24 June 2014, accessed 17 February 2015, http://www.theguardian.com/culture-professionals-network/culture-professionals-blog/2013/jun/24/pay-artists-funding-friction-future.

16   Chris Gibson, 'Negotiating regional creative economies: academics as expert intermediaries advocating progressive alternatives', *Regional Studies* 49 (2014): 476.

17   Schlesinger, 'Expertise, the academy and the governance of cultural policy', 27.

DOI: 10.1057/9781137478887.0009

Appendix

Schlesinger, Philip, Melanie Selfe and Ealasaid Munro. *Curators of Cultural Enterprise: A Critical Analysis of a Creative Business Intermediary*. Basingstoke: Palgrave Macmillan, 2015. DOI: 10.1057/9781137478887.0010.

How it all began

The preliminaries to this project began with an exchange of views in an Edinburgh coffee bar in the dreich days of January 2012, when the film producer, Bob Last, and this study's principal investigator, Philip Schlesinger, found that their thinking about creative micro-businesses was largely on the same page. Both were intensely aware of the challenges posed to precarious cultural work, which has been an increasing focus of academic research.[1]

Bob Last – then Chair of CEO's Board – had begun some research for the Scottish Government on small creative enterprises and the kind of access to finance they had (or did not have) and wanted to run it past Schlesinger. Although the discussion took place well before the historic 18 September 2014 vote in the referendum on Scottish independence, Last's project indicated that an interest in how to capitalise on the creative economy was then already on the Scottish Government's agenda. After their discussion in Edinburgh, an exchange of papers confirmed that the two were indeed thinking on similar lines.

At that time, neither imagined that the present study, which at least in part addresses their respective concerns, would be undertaken. A few months later, however, the opportunity for CEO and the Centre for Cultural Policy Research (CCPR) to collaborate on a project arose quite unexpectedly, when Schlesinger received an invitation from the AHRC to bid for a 'creative economy knowledge exchange' project. Recalling his conversation with Bob Last, Schlesinger proposed the idea of studying CEO to the AHRC. While no commitment to funding was given, he was told that if submitted it would at least be considered. So Schlesinger and co-investigator, Melanie Selfe, worked on the ideas that – by way of a successful application – led to this study taking place.

Framing the project

Without the enthusiastic co-operation of CEO's Director, Deborah Keogh, and Fiona Pilgrim, Professional Development Manager, the project would not have taken the form it did. Over several months, they collaborated with Schlesinger and Selfe as they worked on the aims, objectives and methods, informing them about how CEO worked and identifying issues that might be addressed by research. This process certainly came close to the 'co-production' of this project's ideas.[2] A

DOI: 10.1057/9781137478887.0010

confidentiality agreement was devised to protect CEO clients' interests. And – bravely and most unusually – the researchers were offered largely unrestricted access to meetings, daily activities, and records. We were governed by the University of Glasgow's ethical code in our dealings.

Both Keogh and Pilgrim showed a deep understanding of the potential benefits that outside scrutiny could bring to CEO. Keogh believed that detailed research into its current practice could begin to unlock the knowledge accumulated by staff, who were always on the run. For his part, Bob Last thought that CEO could benefit generally from being opened up to research at a time when he was thinking hard about its mission, himself researching how to analyse creative work to best effect, and also trying to persuade the Scottish Government and Creative Scotland to reconsider CEO's place in the support agency landscape. Deborah Keogh and Bob Last jointly took the risk of opening the doors to scrutiny and publication. It was clear that they thought that the advantages of a relatively long-term, generously funded study of their organisation outweighed the possible disadvantages. Indeed, aside from protecting client confidentiality, no formal risk assessment was conducted. As we have shown already, sustained external critical attention did have several pay-offs for the organisation, so we believe the decision was justified.

Our cooperative relationship was based on CEO's previous, positive encounters with university research and underscores the importance of academics having good networks when seeking access for fieldwork. Track record was also important. Bob Last had attended several academic and policy-oriented seminars organised by Schlesinger during the previous decade and they had also discussed film policy in Scotland. Deborah Keogh had met Schlesinger through his participation in a workshop on Artists as Leaders, part-supported by CEO, some six years earlier. As establishing trust between researchers and the researched is always difficult, there is no doubt that such mutual knowledge of one another's work and of one another's reputations as well as, not least, the ability to get on well, contributed to opening the doors, and keeping them open.

The AHRC grant was awarded in September 2012. Well before the project had actually begun, its very existence had become 'leverage' for CEO's 2012 funding application to Creative Scotland. Deborah Keogh stated that this had contributed to CEO securing a grant from Creative Scotland's Cultural Economy Programme. To assist the bid, the investigators had provided CEO with precise figures as to the value of the award, which was incorporated into the bid as research income to CEO.

DOI: 10.1057/9781137478887.0010

Completing the research team

The next step was to complete the research team. Along with relevant creative economy boardroom experience in Scotland, Schlesinger brought a background in cultural and media sociology and ethnography to the table, whereas Selfe contributed her expertise in cultural historical and archival analysis to framing the project. The former committed one day a week to the research and the latter two days; in the event, given the extent of the work required, both considerably exceeded these commitments. As, given their other obligations, neither could be a fully dedicated fieldworker at CEO, that role fell to Ealasaid Munro, appointed as the project's post-doctoral research associate. Munro, a cultural geographer, had previously undertaken ethnographic research in a Glasgow museum.

The team therefore consisted of a senior, male researcher with considerable experience of ethnographic research and an in-depth knowledge of the Scottish policy landscape and its key actors; a, mid-career, female researcher with skills in historical organisational inquiry; and an early-career, female researcher with experience of organisational ethnography and her own extensive professional and personal contacts in the Scottish cultural and creative sectors. None of the team members was born in Scotland, although Schlesinger had spent the larger part of his career there whereas both Selfe and Munro had moved to the country as children. As a result, all three team members were deeply familiar in complementary ways with the distinctive Scottish political, social, economic and cultural context, and how this related to the wider UK.

It was a considerable advantage for the team to gain such first-hand access to the world of cultural business support. This offered us the opportunity to acquire deep insights as well as to test our views routinely. It also removed one of the most frequent and aggravating pressures on those conducting fieldwork – the desire of the researched for the researchers to rapidly quit the field, letting them get on with their work and be relieved of the pest of unrelenting scrutiny. For us to be so welcome, therefore, for so long, was heartening and singular.

As we quickly discovered, the team was now ideally set up to enable it to work in line with CEO's own internal division of labour: its Director, the small team of managers and the larger team of junior 'floor' staff. The proximity of the research team to those investigated, and the openness and mutual trust that this implied, presented its own challenges, not least regarding how best to maintain analytical distance. The research

DOI: 10.1057/9781137478887.0010

team's regular meetings to discuss, evaluate and triangulate their findings were key in this regard, as these worked as a routine test-bed for the rapidly growing body of research findings.

Such unrestricted access to a specific site offers tremendous advantages for researchers but also creates ethical and practical challenges. We practiced team ethnography, covering all the different levels of a single organisation.[3] The diverse stages of academic career and the gender mix of the team played directly into the accomplishment and management of fieldwork. In ethical terms, we faced the question of what should be revealed when respondents absolutely trust your discretion and we have exercised our judgement very carefully in presenting this account.

To meet the exigencies of knowledge exchange, we created formal contexts for imparting our knowledge to CEO's staff and, because formality alone did really not meet their spontaneous needs, we also addressed numerous unanticipated demands for informal exchange. The permeability of the research process meant that what was originally intended as observation gradually mutated into participation under the pressure of events and the need to manage relationships in the field.

How the work was done

Our organisational ethnography[4] used several research methods, notably document analysis, semi-structured interviewing and participant observation.

The material analysed included:

‣ minutes of meetings and other internal communications;
‣ documents relating to business planning and strategy;
‣ documents relating to the evaluation of both core services and programmes;
‣ policy documents produced on a range of scales;
‣ academic and 'grey' literature.

Semi-structured interviews were carried out with:

‣ core full- and part-time CEO staff, and Board (n=26);
‣ selected members of CEO's specialist adviser team (n=12);
‣ selected CEO clients (n=17);
‣ CEO stakeholders (n=11).

DOI: 10.1057/9781137478887.0010

Some 200 hours were spent in participant and non-participant observation:

- ▶ in CEO's offices at South Block, Glasgow;
- ▶ during meetings of both core CEO staff and Board members;
- ▶ at CEO events;
- ▶ and in advice sessions with CEO staff and clients.

Furthermore, three, half-day knowledge exchange events were held at the University of Glasgow.[5]

Notes

1   Brooke Erin Duffy, 'The romance of work: gender and aspirational labour in the digital cultural industries,' *International Journal of Cultural Studies* [online first edition] (2015), accessed 11 March 2015, doi: 10.1177/1367877915572186; Rosalind Gill and Andy Pratt, 'In the social factory? Immaterial labour, precariousness and cultural work,' *Theory, Culture and Society* 25 (2008); Luckman, *Locating cultural work*; Murray and Gollmitzer, 'Escaping the precarity trap'; Andrew Ross, 'The new geography of work: power to the precarious?' *Theory, Culture and Society* 25 (2008).

2   Kevin Orr and Mike Bennett, 'Reflexivity in the co-production of academic-practitioner research,' *Qualitative Research in Organizations and Management: An International Journal* 1 (2009).

3   Philip Schlesinger, Melanie Selfe and Ealasaid Munro, 'Inside a cultural agency: team ethnography and knowledge exchange,' *Journal of Arts Management, Law and Society* 45(2015).

4   Ann Cunliffe, 'Retelling tales of the field: in search of organizational ethnography 20 years on,' *Organizational Research Methods* 13 (2010); Helen Schwartzman, *Ethnography in organizations* (London: Sage, 1993); Sierk Ybema, Dvora Yanow, Harry Wels and Frans H. Kamsteeg, *Organizational ethnography: studying the complexity of everyday life* (London: Sage, 2009).

5   The first event, held on 11 November 2013, involved all CEO staff, and was a chance for the research team to present some preliminary findings. The second event was held on 13 January 2014, and involved CEO's Business Support team. The third outward-facing event was held on 3 March 2014 and was attended by CEO staff, policy-makers, academics and representatives of creative support agencies from Denmark, Norway and the USA.

DOI: 10.1057/9781137478887.0010

Bibliography

Academy of Leadership and Management. 'Premier Advisor, SFEDI Diploma in Business and Enterprise Support'. Accessed 10 March 2015, http://www. academylm.co.uk/courses/premier-advisor/.

Ainsley, Sam, et al. 'Open letter to Creative Scotland'. Accessed 9 March 2015. http://www.bbc.co.uk/news/ uk-scotland-19880680.

Andersen, Lisa, and Kate Oakley, eds. *Making meaning, making money*. Cambridge: Cambridge Scholars Publishing, 2008.

Armenakis, Achilles, William Fredenberger, William Giles, Linda Cherones, Hubert Feild, and William Holley. 'Symbolism use by business turnaround change agents'. *The International Journal of Organizational Analysis* 4 (1996): 123–134.

Arts and Humanities Research Council. 'Creative Economy Knowledge Exchange projects'. Accessed 9 March 2015. http://www.ahrc.ac.uk/What-We-Do/ Strengthen-research-impact/Knowledge-Exchange-and-Partnerships/Pages/Creative-Economy-Knowledge-Exchange-Projects.aspx.

Arts Professional. 'Scottish creative industries support'. *Arts Professional*, 29 June 2009. Accessed 27 February 2015. http://www.artsprofessional.co.uk/news/scottish-creative-industries-support.

Banks, Mark. 'Moral economy and cultural work'. *Sociology* 40 (2006): 455–472.

———. *The politics of cultural work*. London: Palgrave Macmillan, 2007.

Beaudan, Eric. 'Making change last: how to get beyond change fatigue'. *Strategic Direction* 22 (2006): 1–7.

Billig, Michael. *Banal nationalism*. London: Sage, 1995.

Bilton, Chris. 'Risky business'. *International Journal of Cultural Policy* 6 (1999): 17–39.

Bilton, Chris, and Stephen Cummings, *Creative strategy: reconnecting business and innovation*. Chichester: Wiley, 2010.

Binkley, Sam. 'Psychological life as enterprise: social practice and the government of neo-liberal interiority'. *History of the Human Sciences* 24 (2011): 83–102.

Boltanski, Luc, and Eve Chiapello. *The new spirit of capitalism*. London: Verso, 2007.

Bourdieu, Pierre. *Distinction: a social critique of the judgement of taste*. Cambridge, Massachusetts: Harvard University Press, 1984.

Boyle, Raymond, and Lisa W. Kelly, *The television entrepreneurs*. Farnham: Ashgate, 2012.

Bridgstock, Ruth. 'Making it creatively: building sustainable careers in the arts and creative industries'. *Australian Career Practitioner Magazine* 22 (2011): 11–13.

Burns-Callender, Rebecca. 'Scotland's creative economy shrinks as London sucks out talent'. *The Telegraph*, 28 January 2015. Accessed 17 February 2015. http://www.telegraph.co.uk/finance/jobs/11372571/Scotlands-creative-economy-shrinks-as-London-sucks-out-talent.html.

Bustamante, Enrique, ed., *Industrias creativas: amenazas sobre la cultura digital*. Barcelona: Gedisa Editorial, 2011.

Centre for Economic and Business Research. *The contribution of the arts and culture to the national economy*. London: CEBR, 2013.

Creative Scotland. 'Annual clients 2014/15'. Creative Scotland. Accessed 10 March 2015, http://www.creativescotland.com/funding/latest-information/funded-organisations/annual-clients.

———. 'Frequently asked questions'. Accessed 10 March 2015. http://www.creativescotland.com/contact-us/enquiries/funding/regular-funding/post-application-faqs/in-the-main-sector-support-organisations-are-not-being-included-as-part-of-the-new-portfolio-what-is-the-reasoning-behind-this-decision.

Cultural Enterprise and David Clarke Associates. *Feasibility study: to investigate the need for a specialist business support service for the cultural & creative industries in Glasgow*. Cardiff: Cultural Enterprise and David Clarke Associates, 1999.

DOI: 10.1057/9781137478887.0011

Cultural Enterprise Office. *Project brief.* Glasgow: Cultural Enterprise Office, undated.

———. *Operating plan for 2010/2011.* Glasgow: Cultural Enterprise Office, 2010.

———. *Cultural Enterprise Office business plan 2015–2018.* Glasgow: Cultural Enterprise Office, 2014.

Cunliffe, Ann. 'Retelling tales of the field: in search of organizational ethnography 20 years on'. *Organizational Research Methods* 13 (2010): 224–239.

Cunningham, Stuart. *Hidden innovation: policy, industry and the creative sector.* Lanham, MN: Lexington Books, 2014.

David Clarke Associates. *An interim evaluation of Cultural Enterprise Office Glasgow.* Cardiff: DCA, 2004.

Dawson, Patrick. *Understanding organizational change: the contemporary experience of people at work.* London: Sage, 2003.

DC Research. *Economic contribution study: an approach to the economic assessment of arts & creative industries in Scotland.* Carlisle: DC Research, 2012.

Department for Culture, Media and Sport. *Creative industries economic estimates.* London: The Stationery Office, 2015.

———. *Creative industries mapping document.* London: The Stationery Office, 1998.

Doyle, Gillian, Philip Schlesinger, Raymond Boyle, and Lisa W. Kelly. *The rise and fall of the UK Film Council.* Edinburgh: Edinburgh University Press, 2015.

Duffy, Brooke Erin. 'The romance of work: gender and aspirational labour in the digital cultural industries'. *International Journal of Cultural Studies* (online first edition, 2015): 1–17. Accessed 11 March 2015. doi: 10.1177/1367877915572186.

EKOS. *Summary of EKOS mapping review of three creative city networks: report prepared for Creative Scotland.* Glasgow: EKOS, 2014.

European Commission, *The new SME definition: user guide and model declaration.* Brussels: European Commission, 2005.

———. 'Creative Europe'. Accessed 3 March 2015. http://ec.europa.eu/programmes/creative-europe/index_en.htm.

Fairclough, Norman. *New Labour, new language?* London: Psychology Press, 2000.

Ferguson, Brian. 'Creative Scotland must be "pulled apart", say campaigners'. *The Scotsman*, 11 October 2012.

DOI: 10.1057/9781137478887.0011

————. 'Creative Scotland faces shake-up after artists' rebellion'. *The Scotsman*, 22 October 2012.

Fleming, Tom. 'Investment and funding for creative enterprises in the UK'. In *Entrepreneurship in the creative industries: an international perspective*, edited by Colette Henry, 107–125. Cheltenham: Edward Elgar, 2007.

————. 'Targeting creativity through the intermediary: regional and local approaches in the UK and beyond'. In *Creative industries and developing countries: voice, choice and economic growth*, edited by Diana Barrowclough and Zeljka Kozul-Wright, 275–305. Abingdon: Routledge, 2008.

Flew, Terry. *The creative industries: culture and policy*. London: Sage, 2012.

Florida, Richard. *The rise of the creative class, and how it's transforming work, leisure, community and everyday life*. New York: Basic Books, 2002.

Fyfe, Nicholas. 'Making space for "neo-communitarianism"? The third sector, state and civil society in the UK'. *Antipode* 37 (2005): 536–557.

Galloway, Susan, and Huw Jones. 'The Scottish dimension of British arts government: a historical perspective'. *Cultural Trends* 19 (2010): 27–40.

Garnham, Nicholas. *Capitalism and communication: global culture and the economics of information*. London: Sage, 1990.

————. 'From cultural to creative industries: an analysis of the implications of the "creative industries" approach to arts and media policy making in the United Kingdom'. *International Journal of Cultural Policy* 11 (2005): 15–29.

George, Molly. 'Seeking legitimacy: the professionalization of life coaching'. *Sociological Enquiry* 83 (2013): 179–208.

Gibson, Chris. 'Negotiating regional creative economies: academics as expert intermediaries advocating progressive alternatives'. *Regional Studies* 49 (2014): 476–479.

Gill, Rosalind, and Andy Pratt. 'In the social factory? Immaterial labour, precariousness and cultural work'. *Theory, Culture & Society* 25 (2008): 1–30.

Grey, David, and Thomas Vander Wal. *The connected company*. Sebastopol, CA: O'Reilly Media, 2012.

Gowers, Andrew. *Gowers review of intellectual property*. London: The Stationery Office, 2006.

Hargreaves, Ian. *Hargreaves review of intellectual property and growth*. London: The Stationery Office, 2011.

DOI: 10.1057/9781137478887.0011

Harvey, David. *A brief history of neoliberalism*. Oxford: Oxford University Press, 2005.

Hearn, Greg, and Ruth Bridgstock. 'The curious case of the embedded creative: creative cultural occupations outside the creative industries.' In *Handbook of management and creativity*, edited by Chris Bilton and Stephen Cummings, 17–56. Cheltenham: Edward Elgar, 2014.

Hesmondhalgh, David. *The cultural industries*. London: Sage, 2007.

Hesmondhalgh, David, and Sarah Baker. *Creative labour: media work in three cultural industries*. London: Taylor and Francis, 2013.

Hesmondhalgh, David, Melissa Nisbett, Kate Oakley, and David Lee. 'Were New Labour's cultural policies neo-liberal?' *International Journal of Cultural Policy* 21 (2015): 97–114.

Hochschild, Arlie Russell. *The managed heart: the commercialization of human feeling*. Berkeley, CA: University of California Press, 1983.

Holden, John. *The ecology of culture: a report commissioned by the Arts and Humanities Research Council's Cultural Value project*. Swindon: Arts and Humanities Research Council, 2015.

Howkins, John. *The creative economy: how people make money from ideas*. London: Penguin, 2001.

Illouz, Eva. *Saving the modern soul: therapy, emotions, and the culture of self-help*. Berkeley CA: University of California Press, 2008.

Jakob, Doreen, and Bas van Heur. 'Editorial: taking matters into third hands: intermediaries and the organization of the creative economy'. *Regional Studies* 49 (2014): 357–361.

Jones, Susan. 'What are artists really worth? Funding, friction and the future of art'. *The Guardian*, 24 June 2014. Accessed 17 February 2015. http://www.theguardian.com/culture-professionals-network/culture-professionals-blog/2013/jun/24/pay-artists-funding-friction-future.

KEA. 'KEA selected to advise on the improvement of culture and creative sectors' statistics in the EU'. Accessed 3 March 2015. http://www.keanet.eu/.

Kitigawa, Fumi, and Claire Lightowler. 'Knowledge exchange: a comparison of policies, strategies and funding incentives in English and Scottish higher education'. *Research Evaluation* 22 (2013): 1–14.

Last, Bob. *Creative industries in Scotland: micro-businesses, access to finance and the public purse. Draft report prepared for Creative Scotland*. Glasgow: Cultural Enterprise Office, 2012.

———. *Creativity, value and money*. Glasgow: Cultural Enterprise Office, 2014.

DOI: 10.1057/9781137478887.0011

Leadbeater, Charles, and Kate Oakley. *The independents: Britain's new cultural entrepreneur*. London: Demos, 1999.

Lean Enterprise Institute. 'What is Lean?' Accessed 3 February 2015. www.lean.org/whatslean.

Lee, David, David Hesmondhalgh, Kate Oakley, and Melissa Nisbett. 'Regional creative industries policy-making under New Labour'. *Cultural Trends* 23 (2014): 217–231.

Luckman, Susan. *Locating cultural work: the politics and poetics of rural, regional and remote creativity*. London: Palgrave Macmillan, 2012.

MacCormick, Neil. *Questioning sovereignty: law, state and nation in the European Commonwealth*. Oxford: Oxford University Press, 1999.

Maguire, Jennifer Smith, and Julian Matthews. 'Introduction'. In *The cultural intermediaries reader*, edited by Jennifer Smith Maguire and Julian Matthews, 1–11. London: Sage, 2014.

Mäkinen, Katariina. 'The individualization of class: a case of working life coaching'. *The Sociological Review* 62 (2014): 821–842.

Martin, David, and Mili Shukla. 'Skills Investment Plan for creative industries'. Presentation made to the Joint Skills Committee, 8 May 2014.

McCrone, David. *Understanding Scotland: the sociology of a nation*. London: Routledge, 2001.

McDermott, John. 'Creative accounting by the boosters of creative industries'. *Financial Times*, 14 January 2015.

McFall, Liz. 'Problems in the economy of qualities'. In *The cultural intermediaries reader*, edited by Jennifer Smith Maguire and Julian Matthews, 42–51. London: Sage, 2014.

McGregor, Alan. *Cultural economy support research: final report [revised draft November 2012]*. Glasgow: University of Glasgow Training & Employment Research Unit, 2012.

McGuigan, Jim. 'Creative labour, cultural work and individualisation'. *International Journal of Cultural Policy* 16 (2010): 323–335.

———. *Cultural analysis*. London: Sage, 2010.

Menger, Pierre-Michel. *Le travail créateur: s'accomplir dans l'incertain*. Paris: Seuil/Gallimard, 2009.

Montgomery, John. 'Creative industry business incubators and managed workspaces: a review of best practice'. *Planning Practice & Research* 22 (2007): 601–617.

———. 'Creative industry business incubators'. In *ESRC research capacity building clusters: summit conference 2013 (25–26 July, University of Aston)*

DOI: 10.1057/9781137478887.0011

Proceedings edited by Ben Clegg, Judy Scully and John Bryson, 25–33. Swindon: Economic and Social Research Council, 2013.

Murray, Catherine and Mirjam Gollmitzer. 'Escaping the precarity trap? A call for creative labour policy'. *International Journal of Cultural Policy* 4 (2012): 419–438.

Myerscough, John. *Glasgow cultural statistics framework: digest of cultural statistics, a report commissioned by Glasgow City Council [3rd edition]*. Glasgow: Glasgow City Council, 1998.

Negus, Keith. 'The work of cultural intermediaries and the enduring distance between production and consumption'. *Cultural Studies* 16 (2002): 501–515.

NESTA. *A manifesto for the creative economy*. London: NESTA, 2013.

———. *Mentoring in the creative sector: industry insights*. London: NESTA, 2014.

———. 'NESTA creative business mentor network: register your interest'. Accessed 15 January 2015.

———. *The geography of the UK's creative and high-tech economies*. London: NESTA, 2015. http://www.nesta.org.uk/project/creative-business-mentor-network/full-details.

Nixon, Sean, and Paul du Gay. 'Who needs cultural intermediaries?' *Cultural Studies* 16 (2002): 495–500.

Oakley, Kate. 'Good work? Rethinking cultural entrepreneurship'. In *Handbook of management and creativity*, edited by Chris Bilton and Stephen Cummings, 145–159. Cheltenham: Edward Elgar, 2014.

Oakley, Kate, David Hesmondhalgh, David Lee, and Melissa Nisbett. 'The national trust for talent? NESTA and New Labour's cultural policy'. *British Politics* 9 (2014): 297–317.

O'Mara-Shimek, Michael, Manuel Guillén-Parra, and Ana Ortega-Larrea. 'Stop the bleeding or weather the storm? Crisis solution marketing and the ideological use of metaphor in online financial reporting of the stock market crash of 2008 at the New York Stock Exchange'. *Discourse & Communication* 9 (2015): 103–123.

O'Brien, Dave. *Cultural policy: management, value and modernity in the creative industries*. London: Routledge, 2014.

O'Connor, Justin. *The cultural and creative industries: a literature review [2nd edition]*. London: Creativity, Culture and Education, 2010.

———. 'Intermediaries and imaginaries in the cultural and creative industries'. *Regional Studies* 49 (2013): 374–387.

DOI: 10.1057/9781137478887.0011

O'Connor, Justin, and Xin Gu. 'Developing a creative cluster in a postindustrial city: CIDS and Manchester'. *The Information Society: An International Journal* 26 (2010): 124–136.

Orr, Joanne. 'Instrumental or intrinsic? Cultural policy in Scotland since devolution'. *Cultural Trends* 17 (2008): 309–316.

Orr, Kevin, and Mike Bennett. 'Reflexivity in the co-production of academic practitioner research'. *Qualitative Research in Organizations and Management: An International Journal* 4 (2009): 85–102.

Paterson, Lindsay. *The autonomy of modern Scotland*. Edinburgh: Edinburgh University Press, 1994.

———. 'Utopian pragmatism: Scotland's choice'. *Scottish Affairs* 24 (2015): 22–46.

Prince, Russell. 'Consultants and the global assemblage of culture and creativity'. *Transactions of the Institute of British Geographers*, 39 (2014): 90–101.

Raunig, Gerald, Gene Ray and Ulf Wuggenig, editors. *Critique of creativity: precarity, subjectivity and resistance in the 'creative industries'.* London: Mayfly Books, 2011.

Rimke, Heidi Marie. 'Governing citizens through self-help literature'. *Cultural Studies* 14 (2000): 61–78.

Rose, Nikolas. *Governing the soul: the shaping of the private self.* London: Free Association, 1989.

Ross, Andrew. 'The new geography of work: power to the precarious?' *Theory, Culture & Society* 25 (2008): 31–49.

Schlesinger, Philip. 'From discourse to doctrine?' *Screen* 48 (2007): 377–387.

———. 'Creativity and the experts: New Labour, think tanks, and the policy process'. *The International Journal of Press/Politics* 14 (2009): 3–20.

———. 'The politics of media and cultural policy'. *LSE: Department of Media and Communications Electronic Working Papers Series*, no. 17 (2009).

———. 'The SNP, cultural policy and the idea of the "creative economy"'. In *The modern SNP: from protest to power*, edited by Gerry Hassan, 135–146. Edinburgh: Edinburgh University Press, 2009.

———. 'Expertise, the academy and the governance of cultural policy'. *Media, Culture and Society* 35 (2013): 27–35.

Schlesinger, Philip, Melanie Selfe and Ealasaid Munro. 'The Supporting Creative Business project and the politics of managing ethnographic

teamwork'. Paper presented at the International Conference on
Cultural Policy Research, Hildesheim, 9–12 September 2014.

———. 'Inside a cultural agency: team ethnography and knowledge
exchange'. *Journal of Arts Management, Law and Society* 45 (2015): 1–18.

Schwartzman, Helen. *Ethnography in organizations.* London: Sage, 1993.

Scottish Government. *Scotland's creative industries partnership report.*
Edinburgh: Scottish Government, 2009.

———. *Support for creative industries: roles and responsibilities, briefing 5
February 2009.* Edinburgh: The Scottish Government, 2009.

———. *Growth, talent, ambition: the Government's strategy for the creative
industries.* Edinburgh: Scottish Government, 2011.

———. *Scotland's economy: the case for independence.* Edinburgh: The
Scottish Government, 2013.

———. *Scotland's future.* Edinburgh: The Scottish Government, 2013.

———. 'European Structural Funds'. Accessed 9 March, 2015, http://
www.scotland.gov.uk/Topics/Business-Industry/support/17404.

———. 'Support for creative industries'. Accessed 9 March 2015, http://
scotland.gov.uk/News/Releases/2009/06/18132606.

Social Value Lab. *Cultural Enterprise Office: performance and impact
2013/14 [December 2014 draft].* Social Value Lab: Glasgow, 2014.

Stevenson, David. 'Tartan and tantrums: critical reflections on the
Creative Scotland "stooshie" '. *Cultural Trends* 23 (2014): 178–187.

Scottish Enterprise Glasgow to Executive Team of Scottish Enterprise
Glasgow, 20 June 2001. *Cultural Enterprise Unit [Internal recommendation
document].* Cultural Enterprise Office archive, Glasgow.

The Smith Commission. *Smith Commission report.* Edinburgh: The
Smith Commission, 2014. Accessed 9 March 2015. http://www.
smith-commission.scot/wp-content/uploads/2014/11/The_Smith_
Commission_Report-1.pdf.

SQW. *Evaluation of the Cultural Enterprise Office: a project review and
evaluation report to the Cultural Enterprise Office.* Edinburgh: SQW, 2006.

The Research Excellence Framework. 'The Research Excellence
Framework 2014'. Accessed 9 March 2015. http://www.ref.ac.uk/.

The Welsh Assembly. 'Cultural Enterprise, paper presented to the
Post-16 Education and Training Committee at Blackwood Miners
Institute, High Street, Blackwood on 18 May 2000'. Accessed 9 March
2015. http://www.assembly.wales/en/.

The Work Foundation. *Staying ahead: the economic performance of the
UK's creative industries.* London: The Work Foundation, 2007.

DOI: 10.1057/9781137478887.0011

Thelwall, Sarah, and Yvonne Fuchs. *Fashion Foundry & the wider set of creative industries talent incubators – a sustainability challenge. Report prepared for Creative Scotland and Cultural Enterprise Office.* Kingston: Sarah Thelwall, 2013.

Throsby, David. *Economics and culture.* Cambridge: Cambridge University Press, 2001.

———. 'A new "moment" for cultural policy?' In *Making meaning, making money: directions for the arts and cultural industries in the creative age,* edited by Lisa Andersen and Kate Oakley, 1–14. Newcastle upon Tyne: Cambridge Scholars Publishing, 2008.

Toepler, Stefan. 'Shifting cultural policy landscapes in the USA: what role for philanthropic foundations?' *Cultural Trends* 22 (2013): 167–179.

United Nations Conference on Trade and Development. *Creative economy report.* Geneva: UNCTAD, 2008.

Vinodrai, Tara. 'Constructing the creative economy: design, intermediaries and institutions in Toronto and Copenhagen'. *Regional Studies* 49 (2015): 418–432.

Wuggenig, Gerald, Ulf Raunig, and Gene Ray, eds. *Critique of creativity: precarity, subjectivity and resistance in the 'creative industries'.* Stockholm: MayFlyBooks/Ephemera, 2011.

Ybema, Sierk, Dvora Yanow, Harry Wels and Frans H Kamsteeg. *Organizational ethnography: studying the complexity of everyday life.* London: Sage, 2009.

DOI: 10.1057/9781137478887.0011

Index

DOI: 10.1057/9781137478887.0012

DOI: 10.1057/9781137478887.0012

Lightning Source UK Ltd.
Milton Keynes UK
UKOW04n1014090815

256567UK00003B/20/P